W9-CIJ-760

By the same author

Fire on the Mountain-Top
Bahá'í Holy Days

"A new life is, in this age, stirring within all the peoples of the earth . . ."

THE
BAHÁ'Í FAITH

An Introduction

by

GLORIA FAIZI

UNITY SCHOOL LIBRARY
UNITY VILLAGE, MISSOURI 64065
DISCARD

Copyright © 1971, 1972 Gloria A. Faizi
All Rights Reserved

Revised Edition

Reprinted 1975

Cover Design by Author

Library of Congress Catalog Card No. 72-84825
ISBN 0-87743-051-9

Printed in the United States of America

CONTENTS

THE WORLD CONGRESS

In April 1963, a large congress was held in the Albert Hall, London. Thousands of men and women came to this congress from every corner of the earth. There were Americans, Mexicans, and Brazilians, Africans, Indonesians, and Australians. People had come from all over the vast continent of Asia; and Europeans from Lapland to Spain were all to be seen in that unusual gathering.

As I looked upon them from the balcony, I could see that every nation, every color and religious background were represented in the congress. But the most wonderful thing about it was that all these people were united in their views and were working towards the same goal—the unity of the human race.

For the first time in the history of mankind, people had come together from every part of this planet, not to solve their differences, but to work in complete agreement.

It seemed like a dream, a miracle. Could the various nations really come together? Could the races accept each other as one people? Could the Christian and Hindu, the Muslim and Jew, the Zoroastrian and Buddhist work together as children of one God?

1

The dream had indeed come true; the miracle had happened. These people who gathered in the Albert Hall in 1963 proved that a New Age had dawned upon our world, that the Brotherhood of Man could now become a reality.

I walked among these thousands of fellow men and women between the sessions of the congress and saw that they came from all strata of society. Some were highly intellectual and well-known individuals; others were simple people like Uncle Fred, one of the Aborigines of Australia, or Andres Jachakollo who came from the mountain passes of Bolivia. Among them were well-to-do businessmen and ordinary laborers, those who had been keenly interested in religion, and others who had been agnostics or atheists. Now they all shared the same beliefs and had found a way in which to put their high ideals into practice. They were Bahá'ís.

In the following pages I shall try to explain, as simply as I can, how the Bahá'í Faith started, what the Bahá'ís believe in, and how they work together.

G.F.

Part One
THE HISTORY[1]

THE HERALD

It was in the year 1844, when a traveler arrived, dusty and tired, at the gates of Shíráz. His heart had been drawn, as if by a magnet, to this small city in the south of Írán, and he had come trusting that God would guide him to the Object of his search.

For many long years the traveler had devoted his time to the study of the signs and dates concerning the appearance of a great Teacher Whose coming had been foretold in the Holy Books of the past. When at last the time had come, he had set out to find Him, for he knew that the One to appear would not come as most people expected. The signs given in the Holy Books were symbolic, and no outward show of miraculous events would announce His arrival to the people of the world. He would be born among men, as all God's Messengers had been before Him, and only those whose inner eyes were open would recognize His station. The majority of people would deny Him and persecute Him because He would bring a new Message

[1] For detailed information on the history of the Faith see list of books given at the end.

3

which would upset the accepted standard of His time.

Before setting out on his search, the traveler had retired to a secluded spot to pray and meditate for more than a month. He had rid himself of all worldly attachments and put his whole trust in God, for he knew that without the aid of God he would never find the One he sought.

It was after this period of prayer and meditation that he felt irresistibly drawn to the land of Írán and to this small city at whose gates he had now arrived. As he looked towards the city gate his mind was filled with strange thoughts. Where was he to go from here? How long was this arduous search to last? Suddenly he saw a wonderful Figure. It was a Young Man coming forward to greet him with a smile on His radiant face as if He had expected his arrival. The traveler was amazed. Who was the Young Man, and how did He know he was coming? From the moment he set eyes on this Youth he was stirred with emotions he could not explain. The dignity of the Young Man's bearing and the sweetness of His manner made an immediate and permanent impression.

The Youth welcomed the traveler as though he had been a lifelong friend, and invited him to His home. Unable to resist the charm of the Young Man, and still puzzled over the strange encounter, the traveler followed Him into the city and came to the door of a modest house. Here, in a small upper room filled with the perfume of fresh flowers, the young Host poured water over the hands of the traveler as he washed away the dust of the long journey. And here, in the course of a memorable evening which has been recorded in the words of the traveler himself, he came to recognize his Host as the One he had set out to find.

As the traveler sat at the feet of his Master through the night, unaware of the passing hours, this first disciple of a new Dispensation had a glimpse of the wonders to come. "This night," he was told, "this very hour will, in the days to come, be celebrated as one of the greatest and most significant of all festivals. Render thanks to God for having graciously assisted you to attain your heart's desire. . . . Eighteen souls must, in the beginning, spontaneously and of their own accord, accept Me and recognize the truth of My Revelation. Unwarned and uninvited, each of these must seek independently to find Me."

BAhIUAh's BAB   (DB 61-63)

Within a short while, the first eighteen disciples had, each in a different way, independently sought out and recognized the Teacher Whose advent they were expecting. When their number was completed, they were sent out to spread the glad tidings throughout the land. Their Master told them that He was the Báb (the Gate) through Whom people would know about the advent of another Messenger of God, far greater than Himself, Who would come to gather the diverse peoples and nations of the world together and establish the unity of mankind as promised in all the Holy

5

Scriptures. His own mission, He said, was to prepare the way for the coming of this great Messenger.

To His disciples, as they set out to proclaim the tidings of the new Dispensation, the Báb said: "You are the bearers of the name of God in this Day. . . . The very members of your body must bear witness of the loftiness of your purpose, the integrity of your life, the reality of your faith, and the exalted character of your devotion. . . . I am preparing you for the advent of a mighty Day. . . . Scatter throughout the length and breadth of this land, and, with steadfast feet and sanctified hearts, prepare the way for His coming." HISTORY (DB 92-94)

The Message of the Báb created great commotion. Although He always referred to the One Who was to follow Him, the Báb's own saintly life and beautiful Teachings inspired wonderful devotion in the hearts of thousands of people who met or heard of Him. His Message spread to every part of the country and attracted people from different classes of society. Even the king could not ignore the flow of reports which reached the court, and he decided to send the most learned and trusted of the religious dignitaries of the capital to investigate the claim of the Báb. The great scholar recognized the station of the Báb and sent back a message to the king saying that he had decided to spend the rest of his life serving the new Master he had found.

The majority of the clergy, however, rose in fierce opposition to the Báb, Whose Teachings

6

jeopardized their position and exposed their hypocrisy. They denounced Him from their pulpits as a heretic and an enemy of God and religion. They did not rest until they had succeeded in arousing the prejudice and hatred of the fanatical mass of their countrymen against Him. Many thousands of His followers were tortured to death; and He Himself, after being made to suffer innumerable persecutions during the six years of His ministry, was publicly killed when He was thirty years of age. Calm and steadfast to the end, the Báb willingly laid down His life for His Cause, assured that the cry had been raised and many were now ready to accept the Promised One Whose Herald He had been.

BAHÁ'U'LLÁH[1]

The persecutions which followed the advent of the Báb had not ended when Bahá'u'lláh declared His Mission in 1863.

He was born among the nobility of Írán. His father, a Minister of State, was the first to notice that He was different from other children; but soon others came to see the many signs of greatness in Him. Bahá'u'lláh was still a child when He became renowned for His knowledge and for His extraordinary insight into the difficult passages of Holy Scriptures. People brought their problems to Him, and learned authorities on religion listened to His discourses, marveling at His wisdom. What seemed most strange to

[1] Bahá'u'lláh literally means the Glory of God.

7

them was that Bahá'u'lláh had never had a teacher or entered any school. But it was not His knowledge alone which attracted all types of people to Him. His loving nature and enchanting modesty won the hearts of all who knew Him.

As He grew up, He became known as the defender of the oppressed and the refuge of the poor. He was always surrounded by people, and children were devoted to Him. Though He was brought up in riches and comfort, He showed no attachment to the material things around Him and gave of His wealth freely to the needy. He loved the beauty of nature, and often roamed alone in the countryside.

When His father died, the government offered Bahá'u'lláh the Minister's position; but He refused it. The Prime Minister was not surprised. "Such a position," he said, "is unworthy of Him. . . . I cannot understand Him, but I am convinced that He is destined for some lofty career. His thoughts are not like ours." (BNE 38)

Bahá'u'lláh was in Ṭihrán when the Báb declared His Mission to His first disciples in Shíráz; but the new Message reached Bahá'u'lláh through the Báb's first disciple, and He accepted it without the least hesitation though He had never met the Báb Himself. He was then twenty-seven.

Having identified Himself with the Cause of the Báb, Bahá'u'lláh arose to promulgate its Teachings and share the sufferings of its follow-

8

ers. Before long, all His possessions were confiscated, and He Himself was thrown into an underground dungeon called "The Black Pit" where one hundred and fifty murderers and highway robbers were imprisoned and where the only opening was the door through which they entered. In this foul place, Bahá'u'lláh spent four months, and the heavy chains which He bore on His neck left their mark on His body to the end of His days.

Yet it was in this gloomy dungeon that Bahá'u'lláh became fully aware of the Revelation which was to flow through Him to the rest of mankind. The gentle Báb had been martyred, and many thousands of His followers had by now laid down their lives for the new Cause. The few who remained, homeless and brokenhearted, were being hunted down by their cruel enemies. But Bahá'u'lláh knew that the blood of the martyrs had watered the mighty tree of God's Cause and that nothing could stop its growth until it had gathered all the peoples of the world under its shadow.

After four months, when He was so ill that they thought He would die, Bahá'u'lláh was released from the dungeon but banished from His native land. So great was the love He had created in the hearts of His friends that a number of them voluntarily went into exile with Him. His young wife and two of His children also shared this banishment. The third child had to be left behind with friends. He was so young that no one thought he could endure the rigors of the long and dreadful journey ahead of them, through snowbound mountains in the heart of winter with no proper clothing or food.

Bahá'u'lláh remained an exile in Baghdád for ten years.[1] He had arrived broken in health, destitute of worldly belongings, and branded as a heretic. It was not long, however, before people of all backgrounds and denominations came seeking His presence. They arrived from far and near, forgetting their differences of class, color, and religion, as they sat together listening to His Teachings. At a time when religious fanaticism was at its height, and people of different beliefs never met as friends, in the home of Bahá'u'lláh they came together as brothers, heralding the dawn of a new Age.

This was not to be tolerated by Bahá'u'lláh's enemies who had hoped that the Movement started by the Báb had been uprooted from their midst. They resorted to every means in their power until they had persuaded the government to send Bahá'u'lláh further away from His native country. An order was issued, banishing Him to Constantinople, in Turkey.[2]

On the day of His departure from Baghdád, hundreds of people thronged around His house with tearful eyes, longing to catch a last glimpse of the One Who had given them so much and asked for nothing in return.

Before leaving for Constantinople, Bahá'u'lláh stayed in a beautiful garden outside Bagh-

---

[1] Baghdád is in 'Iráq which was then part of the Turkish Empire.
[2] Constantinople is now called Istanbul.

dád for twelve days. A tent was pitched for Him in a lovely spot surrounded with the perfume of roses and the song of nightingales. His many friends who came to bid Him farewell were filled with anguish at His departure, not knowing what fresh calamities awaited Him and what was to become of themselves once they were left without Him. But their sorrow was not to last, for now, at a time when the world seemed to have rejected Him, the hour had struck when Bahá'u'lláh could lift the veil of mystery which surrounded His station and appear in His full glory. He was, He announced, that Great Teacher promised in all the Holy Scriptures of the world, for Whose advent the Báb had prepared the way and for Whose sake He had laid down His life.

The Declaration of Bahá'u'lláh, made under such unusual circumstances, was a turning point in the history of the new Cause. Now, at last, the promise of the Báb had been fulfilled, the Day of the Unity of Mankind had been ushered in, and no power on earth could stop its progress.

Bahá'u'lláh's exile in Constantinople lasted no longer than four months, during which time a number of the notables of the city came under the influence of His Teachings. Then He was sent still further away—to Adrianople. Here He stayed for almost five years, and from here He proclaimed His Mission to the kings and rulers of the earth, as well as to the ecclesiastical leaders of all religions. He called upon them to listen to the Message of God, to come together to resolve their differences, and to work for the promotion of world peace. When they failed to respond to His summons, He warned them of the consequences of their acts. He foretold the downfall of their institutions and lamented the terrible sufferings which humanity, forgetful of its God and oppressed by leaders drunk with pride, would inflict upon itself. Through this suffering, however, He could see mankind emerging, humbled and spiritually awakened, ready to turn to the Message of God.

The Revelation of Bahá'u'lláh, which had been born in the dungeon of Ṭihrán and declared on the eve of His departure from Baghdád, reached its zenith in Adrianople. The force of this Revelation could no longer be ignored by either the statesmen of the land or the clergy who were its ruthless enemies. In a desperate attempt to crush the infant Faith, whose followers were being drawn from every religion and all strata of society, Bahá'u'lláh was banished once again— this time to the remote penal colony of the Turkish Empire, the prison-city of 'Akká in the Holy Land. He was sent there to die, for it was known that few could survive the rigors of imprisonment in that foul and hostile place.

In a letter to the despotic ruler who was persecuting Him, Bahá'u'lláh wrote:

"O king, I have seen in the way of God what no eye hath seen and no ear hath heard. . . . How many calamities have descended, and how many will descend! . . . My eyes rain down tears until My bed is drenched; but My sorrow is not for Myself. . . . Yea, because I see mankind going astray in their intoxication and they know it not: they have exalted their lusts and put aside their God, as though they took the command of God for a mockery, a sport and a plaything; and they think that they do well, and that they are harbored in the citadel of security. The matter is not as they suppose: tomorrow they shall see what they now deny.

"We are about to shift from this most remote place of banishment (Adrianople) unto the prison of 'Akká. And according to what they say, it is assuredly the most desolate of the cities of the world, the most unsightly of them in appearance, the most detestable in climate, and the foulest in water; it is as though it were the metropolis of the owl; there is naught heard therein save the sound of its hooting. And in it they intend to imprison this Servant, and to shut in our faces the doors of leniency and take away from us the good things of the life of the world during what remaineth of our days. By God, though weariness should weaken Me, and hunger should destroy Me, though My couch should be made of the hard rock and My associates of the beasts of the desert, I will not blench, but will be patient, as the resolute and determined are patient, in the strength of God. . . . Through affliction hath His light shone and His praise been bright unceasingly: this hath been His method through past ages and bygone times."

(BNE 46)

Bahá'u'lláh's followers were once more filled

13

with sorrow at this fresh calamity and cruel suffering which was inflicted on their beloved Master. But Bahá'u'lláh assured them that the prison gates would be thrown open and the Message of God would be taken from the Holy Land to all parts of the earth as foretold in the Holy Books.

And so it was to be. Bahá'u'lláh, His family, and many of His followers who had refused to be separated from Him were made to bear terrible hardships in the prison of 'Akká, but in time, the unfriendly population of the penal colony, the uncouth prison guards, and even the officers in charge were slowly affected by the spirit of the Teachings of the noble Prisoner Who had made His home among them. The orders which were repeatedly received in 'Akká concerning the severe measures that were to be enforced against Bahá'u'lláh were gradually disregarded by those in charge of the prison, and the travelers who arrived from far distances, often on foot, to visit Bahá'u'lláh, were no more turned away from the city gates. The time came when, after nine years of confinement, the highest religious official in 'Akká begged Bahá'u'lláh to terminate His imprisonment within the city walls and go to live in the country where a beautiful mansion had been rented for Him.

Despite the fact that the government never withdrew the prison sentence, Bahá'u'lláh lived the last years of His life under conditions very different from what His enemies had hoped. Once again, a stream of visitors, people of every class and description, came from the surrounding countries to hear His Teachings. And His ever-increasing followers, now known as Bahá'ís, took the life-giving Message from the Holy Land to the world outside.

Among those who came to visit Bahá'u'lláh at this time was the famous orientalist, Professor Edward G. Browne, of the University of Cambridge, who has recorded his impressions of the meeting. He writes:

"The face of him on whom I gazed I can never forget, though I cannot describe it. Those piercing eyes seemed to read one's very soul; power and authority sat on that ample brow. . . . No need to ask in whose presence I stood, as I bowed myself before one who is the object of a devotion and love which kings might envy and emperors sigh for in vain!

"A mild dignified voice bade me be seated, and then continued:—'Praise be to God that thou hast attained! . . . Thou hast come to see a prisoner and an exile. . . . We desire but the good of the world and the happiness of the nations; yet they deem us a stirrer-up of strife and sedition worthy of bondage and banishment. . . . That all nations should become one in faith and all men as brothers; that the bonds of affection and unity between the sons of men should be strengthened; that diversity of religion should cease, and differences of race be annulled—what harm is there in this? . . . Yet so it shall be; these fruitless strifes, these ruinous wars shall pass

away, and the "Most Great Peace" shall come.
... Let not a man glory in this, that he loves his
country; let him rather glory in this, that he loves
his kind. ...'

"Such, so far as I can recall them, were the
words which, besides many others, I heard from
Behá. Let those who read them consider well
with themselves whether such doctrines merit
death and bonds, and whether the world is more
likely to gain or lose by their diffusion."

(B 62)

Throughout His turbulent life, Bahá'u'lláh
found time to write works which would fill over
a hundred volumes. Among them are His famous
letters to the kings and rulers of the world, His
beautiful prayers and meditations, and His spiritual and social laws. Before He passed away in
1892, Bahá'u'lláh safeguarded His Faith from
splitting into sects by appointing His son, 'Abdu'l-
Bahá, as the One to Whom all Bahá'ís should
turn for guidance. He was to be the sole Interpreter of Bahá'u'lláh's Writings and the Exemplar
of His Cause.

THE EXEMPLAR

'Abdu'l-Bahá means the Servant of the Glory. This title, by which He chose to be called,
sums up the life of the Exemplar of the Bahá'í
Faith. From His early days when as a child He
had been taken to see Bahá'u'lláh in the dungeon of Ṭihrán, to the time when, after a life of

16

suffering and triumph, He was laid to rest on the slopes of Mount Carmel, He had but one desire—to serve the Cause of Bahá'u'lláh.

He was eight years old when Bahá'u'lláh was cast into "The Black Pit." All their property was confiscated, and even their friends were afraid to come near them. In the empty house, 'Abdu'l-Bahá's mother put a handful of flour into His palm, as the only nourishment she could provide. When He went out on the street, He was stoned as the child of heretics. Later, He followed His Father into exile and willingly shared all His sufferings when He was banished from place to place, and finally to the Prison of 'Akká.

As He grew into manhood, 'Abdu'l-Bahá came to be regarded as the embodiment of all the virtues that Bahá'ís long to attain. He was gentle and courteous; He was generous and brave. He combined great wisdom with touching humility; and His love for God and His fellow-men knew no bounds. He spent every day of His life serving others and bringing joy into the lives of all around Him. The poor and the sick were His special care, and the orphan looked upon Him as a father. His friends loved Him to the point of adoration, and His enemies could find no blemish in His beautiful character. His station was not that of a Messenger of God, but His life was an example of human perfection.

During Bahá'u'lláh's lifetime, 'Abdu'l-Bahá was His closest companion. He spared Himself no trouble in order to bring a measure of comfort into His Father's life. He took upon Himself the

17

tedious daily tasks so that Bahá'u'lláh could devote His time to more important matters. Many of those who thronged to their home in Baghdád were quite satisfied to meet 'Abdu'l-Bahá and bring their questions to Him, although He was still in His early youth. As time went on, Bahá'u'lláh Himself would encourage His followers to take their problems to 'Abdu'l-Bahá, Whom He lovingly referred to as "the Master."

After Bahá'u'lláh passed away, the Bahá'ís turned to 'Abdu'l Bahá as their leader and their guide. His selfless devotion to the Cause of God was an inspiration to them all. His guidance helped them to take the new Message to different parts of the world.

'Abdu'l-Bahá Himself was still a prisoner in 'Akká. With the passing of Bahá'u'lláh, the enemies of the Faith had found fresh zeal and renewed their attacks on 'Abdu'l-Bahá, Who was once more confined within the city walls. Through His vast correspondence, however, He kept in constant touch with the Bahá'ís everywhere, answering their questions, guiding their activities, encouraging them in their work, and uplifting their spirits when they were being persecuted for their Faith.

Persecutions of one kind or another were inflicted on 'Abdu'l-Bahá Himself for many long years. Through it all, He remained calm and happy. His joy of life and His delightful sense of humor never left Him. "My home is the home of laughter and mirth,"[1] He would say. When peo-

[1] J. E. Esslemont, *Bahá'u'lláh and the New Era*, p. 77

18

ple wondered what kept Him so happy under the most trying conditions, He said there is no prison but the prison of self.

At last, the revolution of the Young Turks set all the prisoners in 'Akká free, and 'Abdu'l-Bahá's confinement came to an end. His captivity in the Holy Land had lasted forty years! He had gone into prison as a youth, and came out of it as an old man. Although He was broken in health, His spirit was unshaken, and, as soon as He had freedom of movement, He decided to take the Message of Bahá'u'lláh to the Western world.

The Bahá'í Faith, which had first spread to the Middle East, the Far East, and North Africa, was now being established in Europe and America. Already a number of Western Bahá'ís had come to visit 'Abdu'l-Bahá in the Holy Land, and gone back fired with enthusiasm and determined to spread the Message in all parts of the West.

'Abdu'l-Bahá's extensive journeys throughout Europe and America, when He was almost seventy, brought the Faith to the attention of millions of people. He was invited to speak at churches and synagogues, temples and mosques, universities and charitable institutions. Thousands of people, from the highest government officials, scientists, and philosophers, to the most humble workmen and poorest tramps, came to meet Him from early morning till late at night; and 'Abdu'l-Bahá gave them all freely of His wisdom and love. They went away uplifted, inspired with new hope, and full of wonder about the Man Who had spent most of His life in prison yet had such an understanding of other people's problems and such vast knowledge of world affairs. Millions of others who did not meet 'Abdu'l-Bahá heard about Him and the Message He had brought to their shores through dozens of articles in the press.

By the example of His life, 'Abdu'l-Bahá showed how it is possible to put into practice the loftiest spiritual ideals under all kinds of conditions and in situations as different as those of life in a penal colony and in the most modern cities of the world.

'Abdu'l-Bahá passed away in the Holy Land in 1921, serving the Cause He loved so well to the last day of His life. He had once said, "Behold a candle how it gives its light. It weeps its life away drop by drop in order to give forth its flame of light."[1] How well this applied to the life of 'Abdu'l-Bahá, Who gave of Himself day and night in order to light the way for others.

THE GUARDIAN OF THE CAUSE

By the end of 'Abdu'l-Bahá's ministry, the Bahá'í Faith had attracted a great number of followers from backgrounds as different as Jewish, Christian, Muslim, Hindu, Buddhist, Zoroastrian, and atheist. They came from various nations, races, and cultures of the world. As Bahá'ís, they now had to learn to work together as one people.

[1] May Maxwell, *An Early Pilgrimage* (London: George Ronald, 1953), p. 42.

In the lifetime of 'Abdu'l-Bahá, they had turned to Him for guidance at every step, and He had taught them and watched over them like a loving father. Under His patient care, they had begun to lay down the foundations of their administrative institutions, the plan for which had been given by Baha'u'lláh Himself. Through these institutions, to be established throughout the entire world, the followers of Bahá'u'lláh, wherever they lived, would be linked together and able to work as one body for the promotion of the spiritual and social principles of their Faith. But the Bahá'ís had just begun to get a glimpse of this unique, worldwide Administrative Order, which was so different from anything they had known before and which was to coordinate their activities and preserve their unity, when 'Abdu'l-Bahá passed away. Many wondered how the members of this infant Faith, coming from such diverse backgrounds, could continue to remain united after the magnetic personality of 'Abdu'l-Bahá was removed from their midst.

But Bahá'u'lláh had promised His followers that His Cause would not split into sects, that no matter what tests and trials beset the new Faith, it would grow in strength and unity until it had accomplished its mission in the world. The Bahá'ís of the East and West, bereaved by the passing of 'Abdu'l-Bahá, found in His Will and Testament the guidance they needed for the next stage of their development. In this important document, 'Abdu'l-Bahá had appointed His grandson, Shoghi Effendi, as Guardian of the Cause of Bahá'u'lláh and had asked the

21

Bahá'ís to put their trust in him and offer him their undivided loyalty.

During the thirty-six years of the Guardian's ministry, the Bahá'ís of the world, working under his direction and in close collaboration with each other, established their administrative institutions throughout the planet on a foundation strong enough to enable them to work together in perfect harmony.

Shoghi Effendi was related to both the Báb and Bahá'u'lláh. His mother was the daughter of 'Abdu'l-Bahá, his father was a close relative of the Báb. In his childhood, his devotion to 'Abdu'l-Bahá was very touching; and when he grew up, his greatest joy was in obedience to 'Abdu'l-Bahá. Though he had already decided to dedicate his whole life to the service of the Cause, the contents of 'Abdu'l-Bahá's Will came to him as a shock. He was only twenty-four at the time and had not realized that he might one day be called upon to shoulder such a tremendous responsibility. At first, overcome by the grief of 'Abdu'l-Bahá's sudden death at a time when he himself was studying away from the Holy Land, and shaken by the extraordinary task assigned to him in 'Abdu'l-Bahá's Will and Testament, he went away to be alone for some time. After a long period of preparation, he came back ready to shoulder his responsibilities as the Guardian of the Cause. From that day onwards he did not spare himself in any way. Content with little food and rest, he worked every hour of the day and far into the night, attending to the many needs of a fast-growing world community.

The detailed plans he gave for the progress of the Faith in both the East and the West; the innumerable letters he answered; the volumes of translations he made from the writings of the Báb, Bahá'u'lláh, and 'Abdu'l-Bahá, as well as the remarkable books he personally wrote, all remain as a lasting tribute to the colossal amount of dedicated work he accomplished.

As a man, Shoghi Effendi had a rare combination of outstanding qualities which set him apart from others and which inspired great love and admiration in all those who knew him. As Guardian of the Cause, he led the Bahá'ís through ordeals which often seemed insurmountable, to victory after victory, until the Administrative Order of their Faith was firmly established throughout the world, the institutions through which they could combine their forces in the service of God and their fellowmen had been erected, and the unity of the followers of Bahá'u'lláh ensured throughout the Baha'í Dispensation.

In His Will and Testament, 'Abdu'l-Bahá had assured the Bahá'ís that the Guardian would be under God's special care and protection and that he would be guided to lead them in all their undertakings. The years of the Guardianship proved the significance of 'Abdu'l-Bahá's promise.

Part Two
THE TEACHINGS OF BAHÁ'U'LLÁH

GOD

Man has always been aware of a mysterious Power in the universe. Sometimes he has identified this Power with things he could see but knew little about, like the sun and stars; sometimes he has thought of the Mystery as an invisible person or a group of individuals very much like himself but with greater powers; at other times he has had more abstract and complicated ideas about the First Cause through which Creation has come into being and whose presence he has instinctively felt or rationally reasoned. People living in different parts of the world have not agreed on what this Mystery is, but on one point they are united: that such a Mystery exists.

Bahá'u'lláh teaches that men throughout the ages have sought after the same Reality though their understanding of it has been different. They have used different names and worshiped in different ways; but they are, in truth, fellow-believers in this mysterious Power which is greater than themselves.

Albert Einstein, the famous twentieth-century scientist, expresses his belief in this way:

"My religion consists of a humble admiration of the illimitable superior spirit who reveals himself in the slight details we are able to perceive with our frail and feeble minds. That deeply emotional conviction of the presence of a superior reasoning power, which is revealed in the incomprehensible universe, forms my idea of God."[1]

Bahá'ís agree with the scientist that we cannot fully understand this "superior reasoning power" with our limited human minds. This is why our concept of God has changed, and will continue to change.

Though our knowledge of God is limited, His love for us has never failed. Bahá'u'lláh says God has communicated this love in every age through a Man Whom He has chosen to be His Mouthpiece on earth. The Messenger of God among us conveys, in terms which we can understand—through His life and Teachings—the boundless love of God for His creation. He comes at a time when we need Him most, though we in our ignorance are seldom aware of our need; and He is prepared to suffer the indignities we heap upon Him in return for the love He showers on us and the guidance He freely gives for our happiness. If we recognize this Messenger of God, Bahá'u'lláh says we have recognized the One Who speaks through Him:

"The door of the knowledge of the Ancient

[1] Lincoln Barrett, *The Universe and Dr. Einstein* (New York: William Morrow and Company, Inc., 1949), p. 106.

26

Being hath ever been, and will continue for ever to be, closed in the face of men. No man's understanding shall ever gain access unto His holy court. As a token of His mercy, however, and as a proof of His loving-kindness, He hath manifested unto men the Daystars of His divine guidance, the Symbols of His divine unity, and hath ordained the knowledge of these sanctified Beings to be identical with the knowledge of His own Self. Whoso recognizeth them hath recognized God. Whoso hearkeneth to their call, hath hearkened to the Voice of God. . . ."

(GWB 49-50)

THE MANIFESTATIONS OF GOD

The Messengers of God are the Founders of the world's great religions. They are not to be confused with the minor prophets, saints, or reformers who have derived their inspiration from the Founder of their Faith. To give an example: Christ is the Founder of Christianity which is one of the world's independent religions. Within Christianity, however, there are now hundreds of different denominations; and the station of the founders of these sects, no matter how important they may be, cannot be compared with the supreme station of Christ, Whose teachings they have set out to expound.

The Messengers of God have appeared at different times in history and among different peoples. Indeed, it would be impossible to think of a loving Creator Who could withhold His guidance from any section of the human race.

These divine Messengers manifest in their own lives attributes of God, such as love, mercy, justice, and power, to a degree far above the capacity of ordinary human beings. Bahá'u'lláh calls them the Manifestations of God. If we liken God to the sun, a Manifestation of God is like a perfect mirror which reflects the light, heat, and the life-giving powers of the sun. The sun does not descend into the mirror; therefore we cannot say that the mirror is the sun, but if we had no other way of seeing the sun, we could look into the mirror and see its perfect reflection. Bahá'u'lláh says:

"These sanctified Mirrors ... are, one and all, the Exponents on earth of Him Who is the central Orb of the universe, its Essence and ultimate Purpose. From Him proceed their knowledge and power; from Him is derived their sovereignty. The beauty of their countenance is but a reflection of His image, and their revelation a sign of His deathless glory. . . . Through them is transmitted a grace that is infinite, and by them is revealed the Light that can never fade."

(GWB 47)

The Manifestations of God have a twofold station. Each one of them is, at one time or another, the Mouthpiece of God on earth. In this respect they are the same, and no distinction can be made between them. Their other station pertains to the limitations of the human world. Each has a different name, a distinct individuality, and a definite mission. When addressing the world,

28

God's Messenger sometimes speaks with the voice and authority of God Himself, while at other times, He speaks as a man charged with a Message from God to His fellowmen. In the words of Bahá'u'lláh:

"Were any of the all-embracing Manifestations of God to declare: 'I am God,' He, verily, speaketh the truth, and no doubt attacheth thereto. For it hath been repeatedly demonstrated that through their Revelation, their attributes and names, the Revelation of God, His names and His attributes, are made manifest in the world. . . . And were they to say, 'We are the Servants of God,' this also is a manifest and indisputable fact. For they have been made manifest in the uttermost state of servitude, a servitude the like of which no man can possibly attain."

(GWB 54-55)

Most people are prepared to accept the Founder of their own Faith as the Mouthpiece or Manifestation of God on earth, but they are convinced that His station is unique and the Founders of other religions cannot be compared with Him. Bahá'u'lláh teaches that the Messengers of God are not to be set up as rivals in the world, each competing with the others for the homage of the human race. They are like teachers in the same school. As a wise teacher adapts his teachings to the capacity of his students, these divine Educators have each given teachings in accordance with the capacity of the people among whom they appeared. The lessons given

29

to a class of small children cannot be the same as those given to older students, even if the teachers of both groups have been trained in the same college and possess the same amount of knowledge. Likewise, the Educators of humanity, though deriving their inspiration from the same Source, have taught what was best for those they came to help.

Many of their Teachings are identical. These are the eternal spiritual laws which are repeated from age to age, and these are the foundations of God's Religion wherever it has been taught. The Messengers of God have all taught their followers to be loving and generous, humble and truthful, to see their own faults rather than the faults of others, and to return good for evil. These are some of those eternal laws which never change, so people living across the world from each other and having no knowledge of each other's beliefs follow the same spiritual standards given to them by one or another of God's Messengers.

Some of their other Teachings, however, are not alike. These concern social laws, such as laws of marriage and divorce, diet and cleanliness. As the people among whom they came lived under different social conditions, each of the divine Teachers gave the laws needed for the time and place in which He came.

But God's Messengers are not just lawgivers. Though they give new commandments and abrogate old laws, they also have the power to change the hearts of men. The grace of God flows through them, and brings new life to a dead world. They open the eyes of men to Truth when they are blinded by ignorance and prejudice, and they inspire their followers with a faith which nothing can shake and a devotion which makes saints and heroes out of the most ordinary human beings.

The influence of the words of a Messenger of God is felt by all—even those who do not believe in Him. For the appearance of each of these Messengers is like the coming of spring which brings fresh growth and movement to the earth and affects every plant with its life-giving power, even those that remain in the shade and never see the sun.

The divine Springtime sets into motion two kinds of movements in the world. On the one hand, man-made dogmas, rituals, and traditions that have been blindly imitated for generations are, one by one, questioned and discarded; and humanity, passing through a state of transition, experiments with all forms of ideas, hoping to find its way out of the chaos which the downfall of the old Order has produced. On the other hand, the standards brought for the new age by God's Messenger gradually penetrate throughout society, and receptive souls begin to echo His words, even if they have not heard of Him. His few followers, who have recognized Him as the Mouthpiece of God, are filled with such devotion that they transcend all human barriers and unite in true fellowship. A new stage in God's plan for mankind is unfolded before their eyes, and, in their eagerness to play their part, they rise above all selfish considerations. Though ridiculed and persecuted at first, the followers of the new Faith grow in numbers until they change the whole spiritual and social atmosphere around them. The unity which is thus established between people who had lived and worked in opposing camps paves the way for a new civilization in which the arts and sciences develop and man reaches greater heights of spiritual achievement.

In the physical world, the spring is followed by summer, autumn, and winter. In the spiritual life of mankind on this earth, too, a cycle commences with the coming of a divine Manifestation, slowly gathers momentum as it moves forward until the mission of that particular Dispensation is fulfilled and its fairest fruits given to the world; then its power gradually diminishes and decay sets in. The cohesive force which held people together is finally spent, and the spirit which the Messenger of God infused into His followers grows cold and dies. His beautiful Teachings which had once united them are interpreted in hundreds of different ways; sects and divisions are formed, each preaching a different message; the letter of the word becomes more important than the spirit; and intolerance, even hatred, replaces love between people who had once worshiped together. Many people, disillusioned by the superstitions and irrational arguments presented in the name of religion, and disheartened by the fanaticism and intolerance they see among various sects, turn away from religion altogether. Materialism, followed by selfishness and greed, creeps into every section of a diseased society; and men sink down to the level of beasts.

At such a time, even the most learned and sincere among men cannot prescribe the spiritual remedy needed for the sick body of mankind. Only another Manifestation of God, reflecting His healing powers, can become the Saviour of the world. When every other door is closed, the Messenger of God appears. He is the only Way, the only Refuge, the single Light in the darkness that has set in. This great drama has been repeated in different parts of the earth, and these very terms have been used in the various Holy Books of the past.

In previous days, however, because of geographical barriers, people living in one part of the planet did not know what happened in other places and followers of each religion thought they had a monopoly of the Truth. They did not realize that God had cared for people living across the world who had no means of knowing about the great Figure Whom they themselves had recognized as the Representative of God on earth. Now we can see what has been happening; but the great religions of the world have, in the meantime, become so distorted by men and have split into so many conflicting sects that it is impossible to go back to their pure source and disentangle the original Message from the interpretation of its followers. Much of the Teachings of the Founders is completely lost. In the Holy Books, expressions are often used which have lost their original meaning and have come to mean something entirely different in existing languages. Other passages are purely symbolic, and people do not agree about their interpretation.

Despite the great conflict of ideas that now exists among people professing different Faiths, there are certain essential similarities between the major religions of the past which are too obvious to be overlooked. They all believe in a Creator, whether they call him God, the First Cause, or some other name. They all have a central Figure— one lone Man—Whose love has changed the lives of millions of people and Whose words are still a source of hope and inspiration many centuries after they were spoken. They all prophesy that there is more to come; and they all promise that in time, when men have lost faith and love has grown cold, a Great One will appear to gather the children of men from the four corners of the earth and usher in the day of universal Brotherhood.

INVESTIGATION OF TRUTH

Bahá'u'lláh is one in the line of successive Messengers of God on earth. Like other Founders of Religion before Him, He has been entrusted with a particular Mission which will guide mankind on a further stage of its spiritual and social development. He is neither the first nor the last of those who have brought God's Teachings to man, but He is the One Who has been chosen to give the guidance of God for this particular age.

The Messengers of God in the past have each given as much as men were capable of understanding at the time, but They have all prepared

Their followers for the day when they would be able to receive more. The time would come, They promised, when the Call of God would be raised for all mankind to hear, and people would respond from all parts of the earth. Bahá'u'-lláh says He has come in fulfilment of that promise:

"Verily I say, this is the Day in which mankind can behold the Face, and hear the Voice, of the Promised One. The Call of God hath been raised, and the light of His countenance hath been lifted up upon men. It behoveth every man to blot out the trace of every idle word from the tablet of his heart, and to gaze, with an open and unbiased mind, on the signs of His Revelation, the proofs of His Mission, and the tokens of His glory." (GWB 10-11)

The claim which Bahá'u'lláh has advanced is no ordinary claim, and He does not ask anyone to accept it without serious investigation. Indeed, one of His most important Teachings is on the subject of independent investigation of truth.

In the days of Bahá'u'lláh, people accepted what they were taught in the name of religion without questioning, as many still do. But Bahá'u'lláh said every man and woman is responsible for what he believes and should not blindly imitate anyone. One of the reasons why people are so divided in their views on religion is the fact that they have been raised in one or another of the many traditions in the world and follow it without thought. If people would forsake their prejudices and investigate truth with an open mind, they would become united because truth is the same wherever it is taught. 'Abdu'l-Bahá says:

"Beware of prejudice; light is good in whatsoever lamp it is burning. A rose is beautiful in whatsoever garden it may bloom. A star has the same radiance whether it shines from the East or from the West."[1]

We can learn a great deal from the mistakes people have made in the past if we stop to think about the reasons why none of the Founders of the world's great religions were accepted by the people of their own time. It was much later that their station was generally recognized, when royal princes and learned philosophers were proud to be known as their followers. In the beginning, most people accused them of being false prophets and did all they could to suppress their Teachings.

Why has it been so difficult for people to recognize these divine Educators when they first appeared? Some of the reasons are these: They have always come at a time in history when a spiritual winter has set in, and very few people are aware of the need for fresh guidance from God. Most people are confident that they can solve their problems without His aid. There are those who have either completely lost interest in

[1] *The Bahá'í Faith: Religion Renewed and the World United* (London: Bahá'í Publishing Trust, n.d.), p. 1.

a superhuman Power or are quite prepared to wait until they die in order to find out if such a thing really exists. In the meantime, they are sure they know how to conduct their lives on this earth without outside interference. Others believe God showed the way men should live centuries ago and provided them with all the Teachings they would ever need to know. They see no necessity for Him either to repeat Himself or give fresh guidance for each age. If there are any further lessons for people to learn, they say, they can all be found in the Scriptures of their particular Faith. The fact that there are hundreds of conflicting interpretations by men who have sincerely set out to understand their Scriptures does not seem to disturb them. There are others, still, who take the signs given in their Holy Books quite literally and expect God to manifest Himself in some extraordinary way with strange and miraculous outward signs. They would not be prepared to investigate the claims of anyone who did not come as they expected. What is more, when the One they are awaiting does appear, He should confirm what they already believe and punish the rest of the world for not having listened to them.

There is little wonder, then, that God's Messenger has always been rejected by the people of His time. He neither appears as they expect Him to, nor does He say what they wish to hear.

It would be foolish, of course, to accept anyone as God's Mouthpiece on earth without being absolutely sure of his station. There have always been false prophets, and there always will be.

What can be learned from the lessons of the past, however, is that we cannot hope to recognize the true Messenger if, for some reason or other, we are not prepared to investigate His claim in the first place, or if, having decided to see what He has to say, we then expect all His Teachings to correspond with our own views.

The seeker after truth cannot afford to set out with any preconceived ideas. He must be completely unbiased and ready to look into any matter presented to him with an inquiring mind, not reject it at once because it conflicts with his own beliefs. He must be fair in his judgment, making full use of his God-given intellect and reasoning powers, rather than relying on ideas inherited from others. Above all, he needs to be humble, for without humility he will never reach the goal. Realizing that his understanding is limited no matter how learned he may be, he will not try to weigh the guidance of God with his own deficient standards. How often in the past the illiterate but pure in heart have had the spiritual insight to recognize the Messenger of God, while the learned men of their age were deprived of this understanding.

As far as we can see, there have been definite signs which distinguish a true Prophet from false ones. The Messenger of God is prepared to endure great suffering for the sake of those He comes to save. His boundless love is showered upon friends and merciless foes alike. His Teachings can transform criminals into saints and cowards into brave heroes who, following in His footsteps, forget themselves in the joy of serving others. His knowledge is far above that of the most learned men of His time, yet He is meek and humble. He stands alone, with all the powers of an unbelieving world arrayed against Him, and rises triumphant from their midst.

If all these signs are to be found in one man, it is wise to take notice of him; for he may be what he claims.

The Holy Books of the past which warn us against false prophets also give us an infallible standard by which we can recognize the true One. We shall know Him by the fruits of His life and Teachings, for it is impossible to gather good fruit from a thorn bush.

SELECTIONS
FROM
THE WRITINGS OF BAHÁ'U'LLÁH

He is indeed a true believer in the unity of God who, in this Day, will regard Him as One immeasurably exalted above all the comparisons and likenesses with which men have compared Him. He hath erred grievously who hath mistaken these comparisons and likenesses for God Himself. (GWB 336-37)

Beware, O believers in the Unity of God, lest ye be tempted to make any distinction between any of the Manifestations of His Cause, or to discriminate against the signs that have accompanied and proclaimed their Revelation. . . . Be

ye assured, moreover, that the works and acts of
each and every one of these Manifestations of
God . . . are all ordained by God, and are a reflection of His Will and Purpose.   (GWB 59)

If thou wilt observe with discriminating eyes,
thou wilt behold them all [the Manifestations of
God] abiding in the same tabernacle, soaring in
the same heaven, seated upon the same throne,
uttering the same speech, and proclaiming the
same Faith. . . . Wherefore, should one of these
Manifestations of Holiness proclaim saying: "I
am the return of all the Prophets," He, verily,
speaketh the truth. In like manner, in every subsequent Revelation, the return of the former Revelation is a fact, the truth of which is firmly
established. . . .   (GWB 52)

Every true Prophet hath regarded His Message as fundamentally the same as the Revelation
of every other Prophet gone before Him. If any
man, therefore, should fail to comprehend this
truth, and should consequently indulge in vain
and unseemly language, no one whose sight is
keen and whose understanding is enlightened
would ever allow such idle talk to cause him to
waver in his belief.

The measure of the revelation of the Prophets
of God in this world, however, must differ. Each
and every one of them hath been the Bearer of a
distinct Message, and hath been commissioned to
reveal Himself through specific acts. It is for this
reason that they appear to vary in their greatness.   (GWB 78-79)

There can be no doubt whatever that the peoples of the world, of whatever race or religion, derive their inspiration from one heavenly Source, and are the subjects of one God. The difference between the ordinances under which they abide should be attributed to the varying requirements and exigencies of the age in which they were revealed. . . . Arise and, armed with the power of faith, shatter to pieces the gods of your vain imaginings, the sowers of dissension amongst you. (GWB 217)

The fundamental purpose animating the Faith of God and His Religion is to safeguard the interests and promote the unity of the human race, and to foster the spirit of love and fellowship amongst men. Suffer it not to become a source of dissension and discord, of hate and enmity. (GWB 215)

It behoveth you to refresh and revive your souls through the gracious favors which, in this Divine, this soul-stirring Springtime, are being showered upon you. The Daystar of His great glory hath shed its radiance upon you, and the clouds of His limitless grace have overshadowed you. How high the reward of him that hath not deprived himself of so great a bounty, nor failed to recognize the beauty of his Best-Beloved in this, His new attire. (GWB 167)

The time foreordained unto the peoples and kindreds of the earth is now come. The promises of God, as recorded in the holy Scriptures, have all been fulfilled. (GWB 12-13)

41

O thou who art waiting, tarry no longer, for He is come. Behold His Tabernacle and His Glory dwelling therein. It is the Ancient Glory, with a new Manifestation. (BNE 37)

This is the changeless Faith of God, eternal in the past, eternal in the future. Let him that seeketh, attain it; and as to him that hath refused to seek it—verily, God is Self-Sufficient, above any need of His creatures. (GWB 136)

Consider the past. How many, both high and low, have, at all times, yearningly awaited the advent of the Manifestations of God in the sanctified persons of His chosen Ones. How often have they expected His coming, how frequently have they prayed that the breeze of Divine mercy might blow, and the promised Beauty step forth from behind the veil of concealment, and be made manifest to all the world. And whensoever the portals of grace did open, and the clouds of divine bounty did rain upon mankind, and the light of the Unseen did shine above the horizon of celestial might, they all denied Him, and turned away from His face—the face of God Himself. . . .

Reflect, what could have been the motive for such deeds? What could have prompted such behavior towards the Revealers of the beauty of the All-Glorious? Whatever in days gone by hath been the cause of the denial and opposition of those people hath now led to the perversity of the people of this age. (GWB 17-18)

Consider the former generations. Witness how every time the Daystar of Divine bounty hath shed the light of His Revelation upon the world, the people of His Day have arisen against Him, and repudiated His truth. They who were regarded as the leaders of men have invariably striven to hinder their followers from turning unto Him Who is the Ocean of God's limitless bounty. (GWB 56)

Leaders of religion in every age have hindered their people from attaining the shores of eternal salvation, inasmuch as they held the reins of authority in their mighty grasp. Some for the lust of leadership, others through want of knowledge and understanding, have been the cause of the deprivation of the people. By their sanction and authority, every Prophet of God hath drunk from the chalice of sacrifice. . . . What unspeakable cruelties they that have occupied the seats of authority and learning have inflicted upon the true Monarchs of the world, those Gems of Divine virtue! (BWF 63)

The Ancient Beauty hath consented to be bound with chains that mankind may be released from its bondage, and hath accepted to be made a prisoner within this most mighty Stronghold that the whole world may attain unto true liberty. He hath drained to its dregs the cup of sorrow, that all the peoples of the earth may attain unto abiding joy, and be filled with gladness. (GWB 99)

Thou art He, O my God, Who hath raised me up at Thy behest, and bidden me to occupy Thy seat, and to summon all men to the court of Thy mercy. It is Thou Who has commanded me to tell out the things Thou didst destine for them in the Tablet of Thy decree and didst inscribe with the pen of Thy Revelation, and Who hast enjoined on me the duty of kindling the fire of Thy love in the hearts of Thy servants, and of drawing all the peoples of the earth nearer to the habitation of Thy throne. . . .

I have no will but Thy will, O my Lord, and cherish no desire except Thy desire. From my pen floweth only the summons which Thine own exalted pen hath voiced, and my tongue uttereth naught save what the Most Great Spirit hath itself proclaimed in the kingdom of Thine eternity. I am stirred by nothing else except the winds of Thy will, and breathe no word except the words which, by Thy leave and Thine inspiration, I am led to pronounce.

Praise be to Thee, O Thou Who art the Well-Beloved of all that have known Thee, and the Desire of the hearts of such as are devoted to Thee, inasmuch as Thou hast made me a target for the ills that I suffer in my love for Thee, and the object of the assaults launched against me in Thy path.   (BWF 89-90)

I swear by Thy glory! I have accepted to be tried by manifold adversities for no purpose except to regenerate all that are in Thy heaven and on Thy earth. Whoso hath loved Thee, can never feel attached to his own self, except for the pur-

44

pose of furthering Thy Cause; and whoso hath recognized Thee can recognize naught else except Thee, and can turn to no one save Thee.

Enable Thy servants, O my God, to discover the things Thou didst desire for them in Thy Kingdom. Acquaint them, moreover, with what He Who is the Origin of Thy most excellent titles hath, in His love for Thee, been willing to bear for the sake of the regeneration of their souls, that they may haste to attain the River that is Life indeed, and turn their faces in the direction of Thy Name, the Most Merciful. Abandon them not to themselves, O my God! Draw them, by Thy bountiful favor, to the heaven of Thine inspiration. They are but paupers, and Thou art the All-Possessing, the Ever-Forgiving, the Most Compassionate. (BWF 92-93)

THE INDIVIDUAL

The mission of Bahá'u'lláh is to establish the unity of mankind. He says:

"That which the Lord hath ordained as the sovereign remedy and mightiest instrument for the healing of all the world is the union of all its peoples in one universal Cause, one common Faith. This can in no wise be achieved except through the power of a skilled, an all-powerful and inspired Physician." (GWB 255)

The unity of the human race is the fulfilment of the promise made by all the past Messengers of God, and must be based on the spiritual

45

foundation which they have laid down and which is once more renewed for this age by Bahá'u'lláh.

Humanity is made up of individual men and women, and to bring about any changes in human society we must begin with its members. Unless there is a change in the life of the individual, the Brotherhood of Man can never become a reality.

In looking at the individual, we see that he was not created to live the life of an animal. When man gives way to his animal instincts, he becomes worse than a beast; only when he cultivates his human virtues, does he become worthy of his name. Bahá'u'lláh, speaking as the Mouthpiece of God, says:

"O Son of Spirit! Noble have I created thee, yet thou hast abased thyself. Rise then unto that for which thou wast created." (HW 9)

Everything in this universe is governed by definite laws. On our earth we see a pattern in the recurring seasons, in the lives of plants and animals around us. None of these can refuse to conform with the laws of Nature. Man, alone, has the power either to obey or disobey the laws which must govern his life. Upon the choice he makes depends not only his happiness in this world but also his future progress when he leaves this life on earth.

The physical instincts which man shares with the animal kingdom are necessary for his life on this planet; but whereas the animal is entirely governed by Nature and cannot transgress the limits it imposes, man can choose to keep his instinctive desires within healthy bounds or to abuse them as no animal ever does.

Man's intelligence can help him to become the master of his environment. Through using his mind, he has completely changed the world in which he lives. But his intelligence alone does not make him any better than the savage; for with the invention of powerful weapons, he can become even more dangerous than before.

Apart from his intelligence, there is a mystery in man which can be related to that greater Mystery behind the universe. In the Holy Books it has been referred to as the soul of man, or his true self. When this spiritual nature of man is trained and cultivated, he rises above the animal world and reflects the attributes of God. Both his physical and mental powers are then used for the promotion of true civilization and the attainment of real happiness.

Let us, therefore, take a brief look at some of those eternal laws which regulate the spiritual life of man and upon which his progress depends.

Love

There are different forms of love. When we are discussing the love of man for his Creator, it may help if we start by thinking of the relationship of a plant to the sun. The life of the plant depends on the sun and its whole being responds to the rays which bring the life-giving powers of the sun to the earth. We may, therefore, say that the plant loves the sun. Man's spiritual life depends on his relationship with God. But as man is not a mere plant, he must understand this relationship between himself and his Creator and consciously respond to the spiritual forces which help his growth.

The plant cannot move into the sunshine if placed in a dark spot. Man, however, has the capacity to come out from a state of spiritual deprivation. But if he is not aware of the necessity for making the move, he will remain where he is while his spiritual faculties grow weaker and weaker until they stop functioning altogether. It is, therefore, essential for him to feel this need in his heart and to learn to "love" God.

The soul of every man yearns for God, as the plant craves for the sun. This is why man cannot find complete inner peace and happiness until he has recognized his need of God and has tried to reach out beyond himself towards the Source of his being. Material comfort and physical pleasure may give him a sense of satisfaction for a while, but he will soon feel dissatisfied again. Bahá-'u'lláh says God is always calling to man:

"O Son of the Wondrous Vision! I have breathed within thee a breath of My own Spirit, that thou mayest be My lover. Why hast thou forsaken Me and sought a beloved other than Me?" (HW 8)

Many people ignore the fact that they are drawn to anything higher than the human plane; others have successfully suppressed this feeling to

48

such an extent that only at great moments in their lives, when the superficial aspects of living have ceased to distract their attention, do they get a glimpse of the important truth that lies buried in their hearts; yet others seem almost ashamed of admitting that there can be any connection between them and God, Who has become an old-fashioned idea unworthy of our modern age. It is true that we can no more bow down to the sun and stars or think of an old gentleman sitting on the clouds, but can we not pay homage to "the illimitable superior spirit" before Whom the modern scientist stands in humble admiration?

Just as the sun reaches down to the plant through its rays, God communicates with us through His Messengers whom we can understand with our human understanding and love with all the devotion of our heart. But it is dangerous to worship the human personality of any of God's Messengers because this will prevent us from recognizing the same divine Reality when it appears with a new name, in another part of the world and under different human conditions. It is as though we were to become so attached to the shape and frame of the mirror which once reflected the light that we refused to see the same light when it shone through a different mirror. But if we are attracted to the divine qualities which set the Messenger of God apart from other men, then we will be able to recognize Him wherever He appears.

When the heart of man is attracted to God through His Manifestation on earth, he has established a link of love with his Creator. And as the link grows stronger, he will feel an overflowing love for all that God has created. 'Abdu'l-Bahá once gave the example of a soiled and crushed letter that reaches the hand of a lover from his beloved. That letter, He said, is no less precious because of the condition in which it has arrived. It is cherished because it has come from a loved one. In the same way, we can learn to love a fellowman, no matter who he is, because he is God's creature.

Service

Love for humanity is the natural result of our love for God. When we love our fellowmen, we will wish to serve them. Bahá'u'lláh does not permit a solitary life of asceticism. He says we should live among our fellowmen, share their joys and sorrows, and try to be of service to them. One of the ways in which we can serve them is through our daily work, whatever our job or profession may be. If we do our work with a sincere desire to be of service to others, it is, in itself, an act of worship. 'Abdu'l-Bahá explains:

"The man who makes a piece of notepaper to the best of his ability, conscientiously, concentrating all his forces on perfecting it, is giving praise to God. Briefly, all effort and exertion put forth by man from the fullness of his heart is worship, if it is prompted by the highest motives and the will to do service to humanity. This is worship: to

serve mankind and to minister to the needs of
the people." (BNE 90)

Prayer

Man can worship and give praise to God
through his daily work. But this is not sufficient.
He should also consciously communicate with his
Creator. Prayer is the food of the soul.

When a man has been starved for some time,
he does not feel hunger pangs anymore, though
his body cannot stay alive without food. The
same is true of his soul. If he does not communicate with God through prayer, he may not feel
the necessity of doing so; but his soul will be in
need of this nourishment to remain strong and
healthy.

In the past, people often prayed because they
wanted something or because they were afraid of
what might happen if they did not offer homage
to a great Power. Bahá'u'lláh says man should
learn to love God and communicate with Him
through prayer as a lover who longs to speak
with his beloved. The mere repetition of words
is, of course, of no value; but when we learn to
pray with dedication, we can draw upon the
spiritual blessings that flow from the Source of
love and mercy.

Prayer in the Bahá'í Faith is not accompanied by any form of ritual. What is important is
sincerity of heart and concentration of mind,
both of which are often gradually attained only
after one has made a regular habit of praying.

In order to teach us how to pray Bahá'u'-

lláh has written many beautiful prayers which have helped thousands of people, though prayer can also be without words. This is one of Bahá'u'lláh's prayers:

"Create in me a pure heart, O my God, and renew a tranquil conscience within me, O my Hope! Through the spirit of power confirm Thou me in Thy Cause, O my Best-Beloved, and by the light of Thy glory reveal unto me Thy path, O Thou the Goal of my desire! Through the power of Thy transcendent might lift me up unto the heaven of Thy holiness, O Source of my being, and by the breezes of Thine eternity gladden me, O thou Who art my God! Let Thine everlasting melodies breathe tranquillity on me, O my Companion, and let the riches of Thine ancient countenance deliver me from all except Thee, O my Master, and let the tidings of the revelation of Thine incorruptible Essence bring me joy, O Thou Who art the most manifest of the manifest and the most hidden of the hidden!" (BP 76)

Bahá'u'lláh asks His followers to pray every day. Apart from the many different prayers which can be used on all occasions, Bahá'u'lláh has revealed three obligatory prayers from which a Bahá'í can choose one for his daily use.

Fasting

This is another of the laws which have been given in every Dispensation. Although it may at first appear to be a physical law—and, indeed, the body benefits much from it—fasting is essentially meant as a spiritual discipline.

During the period of fasting, much time should be given to prayer and meditation; and abstinence from food should be a constant reminder of the more important abstinence from selfish and carnal desires. We should make a special effort to change unwanted habits, to check our thoughts and motives, and to cultivate those spiritual qualities which will make each of us a better person.

Fasting in the Bahá'í Faith is not binding on the sick, on expectant and nursing mothers, on children and old people, and on travelers.

Suffering

Suffering is of two kinds. There is suffering over which man has no control. For example, he may be greatly devoted to his parents; but he cannot guard them against old age and death. His separation from them will bring him sorrow, but this kind of suffering is part of the pattern of his life and necessary for his spiritual development. Bahá'u'lláh wrote:

"Sorrow not if, in these days and on this earthly plane, things contrary to your wishes have been ordained and manifested by God, for days of blissful joy, of heavenly delight, are assuredly in store for you. Worlds, holy and spiritually glorious, will be unveiled to your eyes. You are destined by Him, in this world and hereafter, to partake of their benefits, to share in their joys, and to obtain a portion of their sustaining grace. To each and every one of them you will, no doubt, attain." (GWB 329)

We may not understand the wisdom of suffering in this world, but it is not difficult to see that those who face the tests and trials of life with courage and fortitude grow stronger through the experience. The saints and heroes of this world have all drunk deep from the cup of sorrow.

There is another kind of suffering, however, which is opposed to the plan of God for the human race and is brought about because man disobeys the laws he should be following. War, starvation, and disease are in this category. We should not accept these forms of suffering but should exert our utmost in order to eliminate them. This we can do if we become united in our efforts and follow the guidance which God gives us for each age.

Life after Death

The good things of this life are here for us to enjoy, and we will be no closer to God if we shun the joys of life. We should realize, however, that we were not created to live the life of an animal on earth and be only concerned with our material welfare. We are here for a purpose.

Our life on earth may be compared to the life of the child in its mother's womb. Although in that stage the child is only concerned with absorbing nourishment, it is developing eyes and ears, lungs and limbs in preparation for life in this world. We, too, are here to prepare for another life as different from this one as the life of this world is different from that in the womb.

To enjoy life on this earth in all its fullness, the child needs to develop its limbs before it is born. Otherwise, its progress here will be slow, sometimes almost nil. In the world to come, we shall need our spiritual faculties without which we too shall suffer. But there is a main difference between the child preparing itself for this world, and a thinking human being preparing for the next stage of his journey. The child has no control over its development and is therefore not responsible for the healthy growth of its limbs, whereas in this life we can, and must, consciously prepare ourselves for the next world.

Our bodies are given to us so that we may be able to live on earth while we prepare for another state of existence. When this truth is recognized, we shall stop behaving as though our physical pleasures were all that mattered. The body will not be needed in the next stage of our development, and we discard it on leaving this life as a traveler discards the vehicle which has taken him to his destination. The only thing which will then matter to us will be the condition of our soul which will continue its existence. If we have managed to care for it, we shall be able to enjoy the next world, and our progress there will be healthy and rapid. This is what is meant by going to "heaven," gaining "eternal life," and reaching a state of utter bliss. On the other hand, if we have neglected the necessary preparation while in this life, our progress will be greatly retarded, and we shall be in that unhappy state which has been symbolized as "hell," especially as we shall know that we were given the chance of getting ready for that life, and we refused to do anything about it. We should therefore pay constant attention to our spiritual growth now because it will be too late when our life here is over, and any blessings which we may then receive will be dependent on the grace of God alone rather than on what we could have earned by our own efforts in this life.

When a man wishes to safeguard his physical health, he takes the advice of a good physician; but if he ever thinks of attending to his spiritual welfare, he often, strangely enough, thinks he is quite capable of looking after it himself, though he probably knows far more about his body than his soul. The wise thing to do would be to ask the help of God's Messenger Who is the divine Physician and primarily concerned with the spiritual health of mankind. Unlike the human physician who may not be interested in our case or unable to offer us all the help we need, the divine Physician is fully aware of our condition and has infallible guidance to give. More than that, in His longing to help us He has been prepared to accept every kind of suffering the world can offer. How can we fail to respond to such a Physician and refuse to look into His prescription?

If we wish for spiritual health, it is necessary first to recognize the Messenger of God and then to obey His instructions. It would be foolish to assume that we are capable of curing our own ailments; and having found the One Who can help us, our knowledge of Him would be useless unless we accepted His guidance and put it into practice.

The Messenger of God assures us that the recognition of His station and obedience to His Teachings will bring such joy that, if we could get but a glimpse of this happiness which is within the reach of every human being, we would be prepared to sacrifice all we have, if need be, in order to attain it.

The experience which we call death leads to a life immeasurably richer and more beautiful than we can ever imagine in this world. We should be wise enough to prepare for it and look forward to it with expectation and hope, remembering that God's love is not limited to this life on earth but will surround us throughout eternity. Bahá'u'lláh says:

"O Son of the Supreme! I have made death a messenger of joy to thee. Wherefore dost thou grieve? I made the light to shed on thee its splendour. Why dost thou veil thyself therefrom?"

(HW 11)

* * *

Having discussed some of the fundamental spiritual laws which are renewed by God's Messenger in every age, let us mention a few of Bahá'u'lláh's specific Teachings for the individual in this Dispensation.

57

Work

Work is necessary for all who are physically able. There must be no idle rich, relying on the work of others, and no idle poor begging for their means of livelihood. Bahá'u'lláh writes:

"It is enjoined on every one of you to engage in some occupation—some art, trade or the like. We have made this—your occupation—identical with the worship of God. . . .

"Waste not your time in idleness and indolence, and occupy yourselves with that which will profit yourselves and others beside yourselves. . . . The most despised of men before God is he who sits and begs." (BNE 143)

Acquisition of Knowledge

A great deal of stress is laid by Bahá'u'lláh on the training in arts and sciences and other professions. He says:

"Knowledge is as wings to man's life, and a ladder for his ascent. Its acquisition is incumbent upon everyone. The knowledge of such sciences, however, should be acquired as can profit the peoples of the earth, and not those which begin with words and end with words. . . .

In truth, knowledge is a veritable treasure for man, and a source of glory, of bounty, of joy, of exaltation, of cheer and gladness unto him." (ESW 26-27)

"The reflective faculty is the depository of crafts, arts and sciences. Exert yourselves, so that the gems of knowledge and wisdom may proceed from this ideal mine, and conduce to the tranquillity and union of the different nations of the world."   (BWF 185)

Dietary Laws

Bahá'ís are encouraged to look after their physical, as well as their mental and spiritual health. The effects of the body, mind, and soul on one another are so great, that we should try to keep them all healthy if we wish to enjoy a happy and well-balanced life.

In the past, many of God's Messengers have asked their followers to observe strict rules regarding food and drink; and when we look into the conditions of the times in which they were given, we realize the wisdom of those laws. Today, because we know much more about diet, and have various means of preserving different foods, Bahá'u'lláh gives His followers almost complete freedom regarding diet. The social customs of some people, however, still prevent them from realizing the harmful effects of habit-forming drugs and intoxicating liquor on the human mind and body. Both of these are forbidden by Bahá'u'lláh, except for medicinal purposes.

Marriage

Bahá'u'lláh discourages celibacy. Marriage is

the natural state and contributes to the health of the individual and of society. Complete chastity before marriage and absolute faithfulness to one's partner after marriage are essential. Monogamy is prescribed, and marriage is to be regarded as a spiritual as well as a physical union. 'Abdu'l-Bahá explains this:

"Bahá'í marriage is union and cordial affection between the two parties. They must, however, exercise the utmost care and become acquainted with each other's character. This eternal bond should be made secure by a firm covenant, and the intention should be to foster harmony, fellowship and unity and to attain everlasting life. . . .

"In a true Bahá'í marriage the two parties must become fully united both spiritually and physically, so that they may attain eternal union throughout all the worlds of God, and improve the spiritual life of each other. This is Bahá'í matrimony." (BNE 183)

To a Bahá'í, therefore, marriage is a very serious matter. It should be based on the love of the two partners for each other; and parents cannot arrange marriages for their children as people did in most parts of the world in the days of Bahá'u'lláh and as they still do in many countries today. Nevertheless, the consent of all living parents must be obtained by the prospective bride and bridegroom before their marriage can take place. This brings unity between the

60

two families and prevents people from rushing into marriage because they believe they are in love, without realizing that they may not be suited to each other and that their marriage is not being built on solid foundations. As Bahá'u'lláh allows no discrimination against class, color or religion, parents should not withhold their consent because of any prejudice on their part but should only have the true happiness of the couple in mind.

A marriage which is based on the love of two individuals for each other and blessed with the consent of their parents has a much better chance of proving successful than otherwise. This is why divorce is rare among Bahá'ís. Besides, Bahá'u'lláh censures divorce in no uncertain terms, although he does not forbid it in the case of two people who develop a great aversion for each other.

Cooperation

The individual, no matter how good a personal life he may lead, has not fulfilled the purpose of his life on earth until he learns to live and work in harmony with the rest of mankind.

There can be no doubt that there are good and sincere people among all the many thousands of different groups in the world today who are working towards social or religious reform. But because there is no unity and cooperation between these sincere individuals, much of their effort is wasted. Indeed, the best of people are often seen working against each other in opposing groups.

Among the principles given by Bahá'u'lláh, therefore, are those which must govern society, so that individuals can join hands and work together towards a common ideal. When people accept the Plan of God for this age, they will be able to pool their resources and work together, instead of each going his own way and spending the precious days of his life pursuing what he himself imagines to be of paramount importance.

The individual is therefore expected not only to better himself in this life, but also to cooperate with his fellowmen in bringing about a better society. The principles which Bahá'u'lláh has given for society will be considered further on.

Note: For study of the topics touched upon see list of books at the end.

SELECTIONS
FROM
THE WRITINGS OF BAHÁ'U'LLÁH

Having created the world and all that liveth and moveth therein, He . . . chose to confer upon man the unique distinction and capacity to know Him and to love Him. . . .   (BWF 102)

How lofty is the station which man, if he but chooseth to fulfil his high destiny, can attain! To what depths of degradation he can sink, depths which the meanest of creatures have never reached! Seize, O friends, the chance which this Day offereth you, and deprive not yourselves of the liberal effusions of His grace.

(GWB 206)

Consider the pettiness of men's minds. They ask for that which injureth them, and cast away the thing that profiteth them. . . . We find some men desiring liberty, and priding themselves therein. Such men are in the depths of ignorance.

Liberty must, in the end, lead to sedition, whose flames none can quench. . . . Know ye that the embodiment of liberty and its symbol is the animal. That which beseemeth man is submission unto such restraints as will protect him from his own ignorance, and guard him against the harm of the mischief-maker.

(GWB 335-36)

Arise, O people, and, by the power of God's might, resolve to gain the victory over your own selves, that haply the whole earth may be freed and sanctified from its servitude to the gods of its idle fancies. . . .   (GWB 93)

Whatsoever deterreth you, in this Day, from loving God is nothing but the world. . . . Should a man wish to adorn himself with the ornaments of the earth, to wear its apparels, or partake of the benefits it can bestow, no harm can befall him, if he alloweth nothing whatever to intervene between him and God. . . .   (GWB 276)

The world is but a show, vain and empty, a mere nothing, bearing the semblance of reality. Set not your affections upon it.   (GWB 328)

This is the Day whereon the Ocean of God's mercy hath been manifested unto men, the Day in which the Daystar of His loving-kindness hath shed its radiance upon them, the Day in which the clouds of His bountiful favor have overshadowed the whole of mankind. Now is the time to cheer and refresh the downcast through the invigorating breeze of love and fellowship, and the living waters of friendliness and charity. . . .

Beseech ye the one true God to grant that ye may taste the savor of such deeds as are performed in His path. . . . Forget your own selves, and turn your eyes towards your neighbor.

(GWB 7-9)

Blessed is he who prefers his brother before himself. (BWF 185)

O people of the world! The religion of God is to create love and unity; do not make it the cause of enmity and discord. (BWF 209)

Consort with all men, O people of Bahá, in a spirit of friendliness and fellowship. If ye be aware of a certain truth, if ye possess a jewel, of which others are deprived, share it with them in a language of utmost kindliness and goodwill. If it be accepted, if it fulfill its purpose, your object is attained. If anyone should refuse it, leave him unto himself, and beseech God to guide him. Beware lest ye deal unkindly with him.

(GWB 289)

Blessed are the learned that pride not themselves on their attainments; and well is it with the
righteous that mock not the sinful, but rather
conceal their misdeeds, so that their own shortcomings may remain veiled to men's eyes.

(GWB 315)

Beautify your tongues, O people, with truthfulness, and adorn your souls with the ornament
of honesty. Beware, O people, that ye deal not
treacherously with anyone.   (GWB 297)

We, verily, have chosen courtesy, and made it
the true mark of such as are nigh unto Him.
Courtesy is, in truth, a raiment which fitteth all
men, whether young or old. Well is it with him
that adorneth his temple therewith. . . . (PBL 26)

Be the essence of cleanliness among mankind
. . . under all circumstances conform yourselves
to refined manners. . . .   (BNE 103)

Be generous in prosperity, and thankful in
adversity. Be worthy of the trust of thy neighbor,
and look upon him with a bright and friendly
face. Be a treasure to the poor, an admonisher to
the rich, an answerer of the cry of the needy, a
preserver of the sanctity of thy pledge. Be fair in
thy judgment, and guarded in thy speech. Be
unjust to no man, and show all meekness to all
men. Be as a lamp unto them that walk in
darkness, a joy to the sorrowful, a sea for the
thirsty, a haven for the distressed, an upholder
and defender of the victim of oppression. Let

65

integrity and uprightness distinguish all thine acts. Be a home for the stranger, a balm to the suffering, a tower of strength for the fugitive. Be eyes to the blind, and a guiding light unto the feet of the erring. Be an ornament to the countenance of truth, a crown to the brow of fidelity, a pillar of the temple of righteousness, a breath of life to the body of mankind, an ensign of the hosts of justice, a luminary above the horizon of virtue, a dew to the soil of the human heart, an ark on the ocean of knowledge, a sun in the heaven of bounty, a gem on the diadem of wisdom, a shining light in the firmament of thy generation, a fruit upon the tree of humility.

(GWB 285)

The source of all good is trust in God, submission unto His command, and contentment in His holy will and pleasure.

The essence of love is for man to turn his heart to the Beloved One, and sever himself from all else but God, and desire naught save that which is the desire of his Lord.

The essence of faith is fewness of words and abundance of deeds. . . .

True loss is for him whose days have been spent in utter ignorance of his true self.

The essence of all that We have revealed for thee is Justice, is for man to free himself from idle fancies and imitation, discern with the eye of oneness His glorious handiwork, and look into all things with a searching eye.   (BWF 140-42)

From *The Hidden Words of Bahá'u'lláh*
(God's Eternal Call to Man)

O Son of Spirit! My first counsel is this: Possess a pure, kindly and radiant heart, that thine may be a sovereignty ancient, imperishable and everlasting.

O Son of Spirit! The best beloved of all things in My sight is Justice; turn not away therefrom if thou desirest Me, and neglect it not that I may confide in thee. By its aid thou shalt see with thine own eyes and not through the eyes of others, and shalt know of thine own knowledge and not through the knowledge of thy neighbor. Ponder this in thy heart; how it behoveth thee to be. Verily justice is My gift to thee and the sign of My loving-kindness. Set it then before thine eyes.

O Son of Man! Be thou content with Me and seek no other helper. For none but Me can ever suffice thee.

O Son of the Supreme! To the eternal I call thee, yet thou dost seek that which perisheth. What hath made thee turn away from Our desire and seek thine own?

O Son of Man! Breathe not the sins of others so long as thou art thyself a sinner. Shouldst thou transgress this command, accursed wouldst thou be, and to this I bear witness.

O Son of Being! Ascribe not to any soul that which thou wouldst not have ascribed to thee, and say not that which thou doest not. This is My command unto thee, do thou observe it.

O Son of Being! Bring thyself to account each day ere thou art summoned to a reckoning; for death, unheralded, shall come upon thee and thou shalt be called to give account for thy deeds.

O Son of Spirit! With the joyful tidings of light I hail thee: rejoice! To the court of holiness I summon thee; abide therein that thou mayest live in peace for evermore.

O Son of Man! Wert thou to speed through the immensity of space and traverse the expanse of heaven, yet thou wouldst find no rest save in submission to Our command and humbleness before Our Face.

O Son of Being! Thy heart is My home; sanctify it for My descent. Thy spirit is My place of revelation; cleanse it for My manifestation.

O Son of Man! Many a day hath passed over thee whilst thou hast busied thyself with thy fancies and idle imaginings. How long art thou to slumber on thy bed? Lift up thy head from slumber, for the Sun hath risen to the zenith, haply it may shine upon thee with the light of beauty.   (HW 3-18)

SOCIETY

The humanitarian and spiritual principles enunciated decades ago in the darkest East by Bahá'u'lláh and moulded by Him into a coherent scheme are one after the other being taken by a world

unconscious of their source as the marks of pro-
gressive civilisation.

—SHOGHI EFFENDI (DB XXXVI)

The world, in the days of Bahá'u'lláh, was a very different place from what it is today. With all the many problems facing us in this century, when we look back on the state of affairs in society in the early part of the nineteenth century, we can thank God that those days are over.

At that time, most countries of the world were ruled by powerful despots. Wealth was in the hands of a chosen few, while the mass of people everywhere lived in abject poverty. The appalling insanitary conditions, the terrible diseases that swept through the towns and villages, the utter ignorance of the masses throughout the world, the cruelty with which the underprivileged were treated by their lords and masters, the superstitions and the fanatical religious hatreds that abounded everywhere—all these were signs of the darkness which enveloped the world when Bahá'u'lláh declared His Mission and gave His Teachings to mankind.

The Message of Bahá'u'lláh was not for the individual alone. Though He laid great emphasis on the life of the individual, He also gave many practical Teachings for the reconstruction of society. He called upon the kings and rulers of the world and the religious leaders of mankind everywhere to unite in bringing about the necessary changes. He told them that the plan of God for this day is the unity of the entire human race and that the complicated problems facing the world today could not be solved until its unity was first established. He repeatedly warned them that if they who had the reins of authority in their hands refused to put into practice the principles which God had given for the new age, they would bring great suffering upon themselves and on those they ruled. In moving and majestic language, He addressed a number of individual sovereigns of His day. Others He addressed collectively in His many Writings. To the leaders of the world's different religions who, in those days, had great power over the life of the masses, He announced that He was the One they awaited and called upon them to forsake the prejudices which kept them apart, recognize the oneness of Religion, and lead their peoples into unity.

When both the kings and the religious leaders of the world, proud of their own power and authority, refused to listen to Bahá'u'lláh's call, He, with deep sorrow, foretold the terrible calamities which would afflict mankind and the great sufferings which humanity would have to go through before it realized its own folly and was prepared to accept the guidance of God.

Though none of the great ones of His day was prepared to champion His Cause, Bahá'u'lláh assured His followers that God would, in His own mysterious way, gradually bring about the transformation needed in the world and that the Teachings He had given would, one by one, come to be accepted by people everywhere.

In the following pages we shall discuss briefly some of the principles that Bahá'u'lláh gave for the healing of the ills of society in this age, and for the construction of a firm basis on which a world civilization must be raised.

Compulsory Education

Bahá'u'lláh's Teachings on education are quite explicit. At a time when education of the masses was unknown, even in the most advanced countries of the world, Bahá'u'lláh called upon His followers to educate their children. He said:

"It is decreed that every father must educate his sons and daughters. . . .
"He who educates his son, or any other's children, it is as though he hath educated one of My children." (BWF 200)

He laid special stress on the education of girls because they, as mothers of the future, would have a great influence on the education of their children. But Bahá'u'lláh explained that education does not consist of the mere acquisition of academic knowledge. Children should also be taught the spiritual standards and great attention should be paid to the training of their character:

"Schools must first train the children in the principles of religion. . . ; but this in such a measure that it may not injure the children by resulting in ignorant fanaticism and bigotry."
(PBL 25)

When the parents are unable to afford the

71

education of their children, the community should pay through the public fund.

Equal Rights for Men and Women

The Bahá'í Faith teaches that men and women are equal in the sight of God and neither sex is superior to the other. Each has something to contribute towards the advancement of the world, and both men and women should enjoy equal privileges in society.

In the past, humanity suffered because women were treated as though inferior and were not given the chance of developing their abilities. When women have equal opportunity of education, they, too, will be able to cultivate their potential talents and offer their full share to the progress of mankind. Speaking on this subject 'Abdu'l-Bahá said:

"The world in the past has been ruled by force, and man has dominated over woman by reason of his more forceful and aggressive qualities both of body and mind. But the balance is already shifting; force is losing its dominance, and mental alertness, intuition, and the spiritual qualities of love and service, in which woman is strong, are gaining ascendancy. Hence the new age will be an age less masculine and more permeated with the feminine ideals, or, to speak more exactly, will be an age in which the masculine and feminine elements of civilization will be more evenly balanced."

(BNE 156)

Universal Language

Among the Teachings of Bahá'u'lláh is that a language should either be invented or chosen from existing languages, to be taught as a second language in schools all over the world. Every child will then learn, besides his native tongue, the universal language by which he will be able to communicate with all members of the human race. Bahá'u'lláh wrote:

"The day is approaching when all the peoples of the world will have adopted one universal language and one common script. When this is achieved, to whatsoever city a man may journey, it shall be as if he were entering his own home."

(BR 76)

The Bahá'í Faith aims at unity in diversity. The different languages and cultures of the world should each maintain their individuality, but there must be a common link between them which can bring about complete understanding.

Religion and Science

One of the important principles given by Bahá'u'lláh is that true religion and true science are always in agreement. This Teaching was given at a time when fierce conflict raged between churchmen and scientists, and people were forced to take sides with one or the other.

According to the Bahá'í Faith, true religion can never be opposed to scientific facts; and

God, Who has given man the gift of the intellect, does not expect him to lay it aside when investigating religious truth. Scientific theories have not always proved to be right, but this does not mean that one should accept ideas contrary to all logic and reason because they are advanced in the name of religion.

Science, as well as religion, has been greatly abused at times; but true science which discovers the laws of the universe and helps our material and mental advancement can never be opposed to true religion which reveals spiritual truths.

Bahá'ís are taught to look upon science and religion as the two wings of humanity. Unless both wings are strong, we cannot soar to any heights of progress. Science provides us with tools and means; religion teaches us how to use them to our best advantage. Science without religion leads to materialism and destruction; religion without science breeds fanaticism and superstition. 'Abdu'l-Bahá says:

"When religion, shorn of its superstitions, traditions and unintelligent dogmas, shows its conformity with science, then there will be a great unifying, cleansing force in the world, which will sweep before it all wars, disagreements, discords and struggles, and then will mankind be united in the power of the love of God."   (BNE 214)

Limitation of Wealth and Poverty

Absolute equality, as far as riches are concerned, is impossible because people's capacities and tastes are different. The order of the world would be upset if we were all forced to live alike. But Bahá'u'lláh teaches that society must not permit extremes of either wealth or poverty. Regarding this matter, He has given certain general economic principles, which, like so many of His other Teachings, are gradually being accepted by many thoughtful people.

Mention has already been made of the importance of work for every able-bodied individual. To a Bahá'í, work is a religious obligation, and when it is done in the spirit of service to others, it is considered as worship. Society must allow no idle rich, or poor, to live on the fruits of other people's labors.

Bahá'u'lláh teaches the principle of graduated taxation. When a person is earning just enough to afford a comfortable life, he should not be taxed; but if his income exceeds his needs, he should pay into the public fund, the percentage of tax increasing as the surplus over his necessary expenditure increases. On the other hand, if a man, due to illness, a bad harvest, or some other reason for which he is not responsible, is unable to provide the necessary means of comfort for himself and his family, he should be helped out of the public fund. No human being should be permitted to live below a certain standard.

Bahá'u'lláh has also laid down certain rules regarding capital and labor. He states that a laborer should receive, besides his wages, a percentage of the profits of capital. 'Abdu'l-Bahá explains thus:

"The owners of properties, mines and factories, should share their incomes with their employees, and give a fairly certain percentage of their profits to their workingmen, in order that the employees should receive, beside their wages, some of the general income of the factory, so that the employee may strive with his soul in the work."   (BNE 153)

The governments of the world must organize a special body of people to look into this matter, taking into full consideration the rights of both the laborers and the capitalists:

"These must plan with wisdom and power, so that neither the capitalists suffer enormous losses, nor the laborers become needy. In the utmost moderation they should make the law, then announce to the public that the rights of the working people are to be effectively preserved; also the rights of the capitalists are to be protected. When such a general law is adopted, by the will of both sides, should a strike occur, all the governments of the world should collectively resist it."   (BNE 153)

Although social laws are necessary for the regulation of wealth, Bahá'u'lláh teaches that the economic problem is essentially a spiritual one. When there is starvation through poverty among people, it is a sure sign that there is tyranny somewhere. The rich must become willing to give voluntarily of their abundance through love and compassion for their fellowmen, not because they are forced to do so. When people become aware of the spiritual values of life and feel a genuine bond of unity with the rest of mankind, they will not wish to amass riches while others are in need.

'Abdu'l-Bahá assures us that this voluntary sharing of wealth will become a reality:

"It will not be possible in the future for men to amass great fortunes by the labors of others. The rich will willingly divide. They will come to this gradually, naturally, by their own volition. It will never be accomplished by war and bloodshed." (BNE 152)

World Commonwealth

Over a century ago, Bahá'u'lláh called upon the kings and rulers of the world to settle their differences and work together for the welfare of the entire human race. He told them that the day for building great nations and empires had come to an end.

Mankind, He taught, has passed through the stages of forming the tribe, the city-state, and the nation. The time has now come for the establishment of a world commonwealth. In an age when it was necessary to unite warring tribes and clans into a nation, love for one's country was meritorious and considered the highest form of loyalty. Today, when extreme nationalism is barring the way to the unity of mankind, Bahá'u'lláh says:

"It is not his to boast who loveth his country, but it is his who loveth the world."   (GWB 95)

In the new World Order, there can be no weak nations. The peoples of the earth will meet as equals. Their governments will each be represented in a world parliament which will be concerned with the prosperity of all nations and the happiness of all mankind.

The world commonwealth of the future will preserve the autonomy of each nation and safeguard the personal freedom of individuals, but it will require the governments of the world to give up the right of maintaining armaments except for the purpose of keeping order within their boundaries.

A world executive, backed by an international force, will carry out the laws necessary for satisfying the needs and adjusting the relationships between nations; and a world tribunal will settle any disputes which may arise, even when the parties concerned did not ask for intervention.

The vast resources of the planet will be tapped and pooled for the benefit of all the people of the world; and a uniform system of currency, weights, and measures will simplify and facilitate intercourse among nations.

Humanity, united and freed from the curse of war, will spend the enormous means and energies at its disposal towards such ends as the raising of the standard of living, the advancement of education, the elimination of disease, the development of science, the cultivation of the arts, and the progress of mankind's spiritual as well as material life on earth.

A world civilization will thus come into being, towards which every race and nation will contribute its best.

World Peace

When the people of the world accept the truth of God's Message and consciously work towards building a new society founded on the spiritual and social laws He has given for this day, "The Most Great Peace" will come, and that Golden Age of peace and justice foretold by the Messengers of the past will be ushered in.

Before that time, however, Bahá'u'lláh foretold that the means of warfare would reach such terrible proportions that the governments of the world would be forced to come to some agreement regarding the abolition of war. When this stage is reached, He said, "The Lesser Peace" will be established—a peace which will serve as an introduction to the time when God's Plan for mankind will be accepted in its entirety and His rule on earth will be universally recognized.

* * *

If we wish to understand the full significance of Bahá'u'lláh's Message and the impact it has had on the world within the past hundred years, we should remember the time in which His Teachings were given and see how far we have come.

Bahá'u'lláh Himself assured His followers that material means, as well as political and economic necessity, would soon pave the way towards world unity. The invention of modern means of travel and communication within almost a lifetime have now removed all physical barriers in the world; the necessity for international understanding is generally accepted; and the great dependence of nations on each other's help and cooperation has already forced us to establish a form of international organization, even though it is but a feeble step towards the establishment of the World Commonwealth envisaged by Bahá'u'lláh.

But humanity as a whole is still unaware of its glorious destiny and is clinging to the ideals of an age which is past. The result, as Bahá'u'lláh repeatedly foretold, is disastrous. The wars and catastrophes that have, one after another, overtaken us in such swift succession ever since Bahá'u'llá's warnings have not yet opened our eyes to the truth of the situation. Terrible calamities, He said, will continue to torment the world until such time as we turn our faces to God and learn to put our trust in Him.

SELECTIONS
FROM
THE WRITINGS OF BAHÁ'U'LLÁH

The earth is but one country, and mankind its citizens. (GWB 250)

The tabernacle of unity hath been raised; regard ye not one another as strangers. Ye are the fruits of one tree, and the leaves of one branch.
(GWB 218)

O contending peoples and kindreds of the earth! Set your faces towards unity, and let the radiance of its light shine upon you. Gather ye together, and for the sake of God resolve to root out whatever is the source of contention amongst you.
(GWB 217)

All men have been created to carry forward in ever-advancing civilization. . . . To act like the beasts of the field is unworthy of man. Those virtues that befit his dignity are forbearance, mercy, compassion and loving-kindness towards all the peoples and kindreds of the earth.
(GWB 215)

The followers of sincerity and faithfulness must consort with all the people of the world with joy and fragrance; for association is always conducive to union and harmony, and union and harmony are the cause of the order of the world and the life of nations.
(BWF 168)

That one indeed is a man who, today, dedicateth himself to the service of the entire human race.
(GWB 250)

The vitality of men's belief in God is dying out in every land; nothing short of His wholesome medicine can ever restore it. The corrosion of ungodliness is eating into the vitals of human society; what else but the Elixir of His potent Revelation can cleanse and revive it?

(GWB 200)

The All-Knowing Physician hath His finger on the pulse of mankind. He perceiveth the disease, and prescribeth in His unerring wisdom, the remedy. Every age hath its own problem. . . . The remedy the world needeth in its present-day afflictions can never be the same as that which a subsequent age may require. Be anxiously concerned with the needs of the age ye live in, and center your deliberations on its exigencies and requirements.

(BWF 36)

Witness how the world is being afflicted with a fresh calamity every day. Its tribulation is continually deepening. . . . Its sickness is approaching the stage of utter hopelessness, inasmuch as the true Physician is debarred from administering the remedy, whilst unskilled practitioners are regarded with favor, and are accorded full freedom to act.

(BR 38)

It is incumbent upon them who are in authority to exercise moderation in all things. Whatsoever passeth beyond the limits of moderation will cease to exert a beneficial influence. Consider for instance such things as liberty, civilization and the like. However much men of understanding may favorably regard them, they will, if carried to excess, exercise a pernicious influence upon men. . . . How long will humanity persist in its waywardness? How long will injustice continue? How long is chaos and confusion to reign amongst men? How long will discord agitate the face of society? The winds of despair are, alas, blowing from every direction. . . . The signs of impending convulsions and chaos can now be discerned, inasmuch as the prevailing order appeareth to be lamentably defective.

(GWB 216)

The time must come when the imperative necessity for the holding of a vast, an all-embracing assemblage of men will be universally realized. The rulers and kings of the earth must needs attend it, and, participating in its deliberations, must consider such ways and means as will lay the foundations of the world's Great Peace amongst men. Such a peace demandeth that the Great Powers should resolve, for the sake of the tranquillity of the peoples of the earth, to be fully reconciled among themselves. Should any king take up arms against another, all should unitedly arise and prevent him. If this be done, the nations of the world will no longer require any armaments, except for the purpose of preserving the security of their realms and of maintaining internal order within their territories. This will ensure the peace and composure of every people, government and nation.

(GWB 249)

O ye the elected representatives of the people in every land! Take ye counsel together, and let your concern be only for that which profiteth mankind, and bettereth the condition thereof, if ye be of them that scan heedfully.   (GWB 254)

Lay not aside the fear of God, O kings of the earth, and beware that ye transgress not the bounds which the Almighty hath fixed. . . . Be vigilant, that ye may not do injustice to anyone, be it to the extent of a grain of mustard seed. . . .
Compose your differences, and reduce your armaments, that the burden of your expenditures may be lightened. . . . Fear ye God, and take heed not to outstrip the bounds of moderation, and be numbered among the extravagant. . . .
. . . Rest not on your power, your armies, and treasures. Put your whole trust and confidence in God, Who hath created you, and seek ye His help in all your affairs. . . .
Know ye that the poor are the trust of God in your midst. Watch that ye betray not His trust, that ye deal not unjustly with them. . . .
If ye pay no heed unto the counsels which . . . We have revealed in this Tablet, Divine chastisement shall assail you from every direction, and the sentence of His justice shall be pronounced against you. . . . Have mercy on yourselves and on those beneath you.   (GWB 250-52)

The One true God beareth Me witness, and His creatures will testify, that not for a moment did I allow Myself to be hidden from the eyes of men, nor did I consent to shield My person from their injury. . . . My object is none other than the betterment of the world and the tranquillity of its peoples. The well-being of mankind, its peace and security, are unattainable unless and until its unity is firmly established. This unity can never be achieved so long as the counsels which the Pen of the Most High hath revealed are suffered to pass unheeded. (GWB 286)

God grant that the light of unity may envelop the whole earth, and that the seal, "the Kingdom is God's", may be stamped upon the brow of all its peoples. (GWB 11)

Part Three
BAHÁ'Í ADMINISTRATION

Soon will the present-day order be rolled up, and a new one spread out in its stead.
— BAHÁ'U'LLÁH (GWB 7)

The call to Unity had been raised. The gentle Báb, the young Herald of a new Age, had laid down His life to prepare the way for it. Bahá'u'lláh, Who was destined to be the Bearer of its message, suffered every form of humiliation and persecution that two despotic monarchs and the host of their powerful clergy could heap upon Him. Over twenty thousand men and women were tortured to death for believing in the new Cause and breaking away from age-old superstitions and prejudices which kept them apart from their fellowmen. And 'Abdu'l-Bahá, Who was acclaimed as the embodiment of human virtues by all who knew Him throughout the East and the West, was forced to spend most of His precious life in prison for being the fearless champion of the cause of unity.

Faced with every kind of opposition at its birth, the Message of Bahá'u'lláh gradually took root in the hearts of men and women throughout the various countries of the world. People who had looked on with despair at the innumerable political, racial, and religious barriers which divided mankind and had given up all hope of true unity found in the Teachings of Bahá'u'lláh a Message which filled them with hope and inspired them to action. And less than a century after Bahá'u'lláh had declared His Mission to the world, a Crowned Head was moved to write:

"If ever the name of Bahá'u'lláh or 'Abdu'l-Bahá comes to your attention, do not put their writings from you. Search out their Books, and let their glorious, peace-bringing, love-creating words and lessons sink into your hearts as they have into mine. . . .[1]

"The Bahá'í teaching brings peace and understanding.

"It is like a wide embrace gathering together all those who have long searched for words of hope."[2]

This "wide embrace" has now gathered together people from every nation, race, and religion of the world and united them in one common belief. Bahá'u'lláh calls upon them to prove their faith, not by words, but by deeds:

"Of all men the most negligent is he that disputeth idly and seeketh to advance himself over his brother. Say, O brethren! Let deeds, not words, be your adorning."   (HW 23-24)

[1] Queen Marie of Rumania (From the *Toronto Daily Star*, May 4, 1926).
[2] Written in 1934, and published in *Appreciations of the Bahá'í Faith* (Wilmette, Ill.: Bahá'í Publishing Committee, 1947), p. 13.

If the rest of the world refused to bestir itself and work towards unity, the followers of Bahá'u'lláh were left in no doubt regarding the task ahead of them. They had to build up their institutions on local, national, and international levels and work together as one unified body.

The principles of Bahá'í Administration are laid down by Bahá'u'lláh Himself, so the system cannot be compared with other religious organizations whose followers decided on the pattern of their institutions after the Founder of their Faith had passed away.

There is one other important feature of the Bahá'í Faith which is different from any other— Bahá'u'lláh, during His own lifetime, appointed 'Abdu'l-Bahá as the "Center of His Covenant." He explicitly stated, in writing, that after His own passing all His followers should turn to 'Abdu'l-Bahá for guidance on any matter which was not clear to them. While Bahá'ís are always encouraged to discuss the Teachings of their Faith and express their individual views on any subject, no Bahá'í, no matter how learned or saintly he may be, has the right to state that his own views are the only right views and expect his fellow-believers to accept his interpretation of Bahá'u'lláh's Teachings. 'Abdu'l-Bahá alone was given the authority to expound or interpret the Writings of Bahá'u'lláh. In this way, the Bahá'í Faith was safeguarded against splitting into sects and schisms.

'Abdu'l-Bahá, in His Will and Testament, made a similar Covenant with the Bahá'ís of the world. After Him, they were to accept the Administrative Order of Bahá'u'lláh and turn to Shoghi Effendi as the Guardian of the Cause. Other measures for safeguarding the unity of the Bahá'í Faith are also taken by both Bahá'u'lláh and 'Abdu'l-Bahá, and these will be discussed as we look into the various functions of Bahá'í institutions.

The preliminary foundations of these institutions were laid down in the days of 'Abdu'l-Bahá, but it was under the direction of the Guardian that they were firmly established throughout the world. In the following pages we will take a close look at the way Bahá'ís join hands to work together towards the ideals they all believe in.

* * *

The Bahá'í Administrative Order, as it expands and consolidates itself, will come to be regarded not only as the nucleus but as the very pattern of the New World Order, destined to embrace, in the fullness of time, the whole of mankind.

—SHOGHI EFFENDI (PBA 1)

Religion without Clergy

Bahá'u'lláh said the day for professional priesthood is past. In former times it was necessary for a group of people to specialize in administering the religious affairs of the community, and the sincere efforts of many selfless and devoted monks and priests who dedicated their lives to helping the uneducated masses and acquainting them with their religious obligations are not to be forgotten or belittled. The requirements of this age, however, differ from those of past ages. Today, every individual should receive a sound moral and academic education, be encouraged to look into religious teachings with an unbiased mind, and accept full responsibility for his own beliefs and actions.

In the Bahá'í Faith, therefore, there is no professional priesthood. Every member, man or woman, is called upon to contribute his or her share in conducting the affairs of the community. Such duties as the performance of the Bahá'í marriage ceremony and the carrying out of official burial rites are discharged under the auspices of Spiritual Assemblies.

The Local Spiritual Assembly

In every locality where there are nine Bahá'ís who have reached the age of twenty-one, they form their Local Spiritual Assembly. If there are more than this number, nine members are elected annually by secret ballot. Every Bahá'í of twenty-one years and above, man or woman, can vote and be elected to the Assembly.

No one can be nominated for membership, and even close friends, or husband and wife, are not allowed to influence one another's views on whom they should elect. During the year, Bahá'ís have ample opportunity for getting to know each other; and at the time of elections each individual should, in a sincere and prayerful attitude, carefully consider who he feels would be best suited to serve on the Local Assembly.

Bahá'ís all over the world form or elect their Local Spiritual Assemblies on April 21, which is celebrated as the day Bahá'u'lláh declared His Mission.

Duties of the Spiritual Assembly

We should always bear in mind that Bahá'í Administration is a means through which the spiritual aims and principles of Bahá'u'lláh must find expression in the world. The elected representatives of the Bahá'ís in every locality, therefore, have a sacred obligation towards humanity as a whole. Among their duties are to provide ways and means for bringing the Message of Bahá'u'lláh to the attention of those who have not heard of it; to safeguard the Faith against people who may wish to misinterpret its teachings; to promote love and unity among the members of their community; to extend their help to the poor, the sick, the disabled, the orphan, and the widow, with no regard to color, caste, and creed; to promote the material and spiritual enlightenment of young people; to provide the means for the education of children; to maintain regular correspondence with other Bahá'í centers throughout the world, exchange with them news of their activities, and share the glad tidings they receive with all their fellow-workers; to encourage and stimulate the development of various Bahá'í publications; to arrange regular meetings of Bahá'ís, and organize gatherings for the purpose of promoting the social, intellectual, and spiritual interests of their fellowmen.

These are some of the important obligations of every Spiritual Assembly. In many localities where the Faith has sufficiently expanded, the Assembly may require the help of various committees. These committees are appointed by the Assembly from among the Bahá'ís in the local community. The Assembly outlines the task of each committee and supervises the work it does. Bahá'í youth under the age of twenty-one can serve on committees.

The Members of the Assembly

The members of the Assembly have important duties to perform but no special privileges within the community. When explaining the attitude and responsibility of the members of the Assembly, the Guardian wrote:

"Their function is not to dictate, but to consult, and consult not only among themselves, but as much as possible with the Friends [Bahá'ís] whom they represent. They must regard themselves in no other light but that of chosen instruments for a more efficient and dignified presentation of the Cause of God. They should never be led to suppose that they are the central ornaments of the body of the Cause, intrinsically superior to others in capacity or merit, and sole promoters of its teachings and principles. They should approach their task with extreme humility, and endeavor, by their open-mindedness, their high sense of justice and duty, their candor, their modesty, their entire devotion to the welfare and interests of the Friends, the Cause, and humanity, to win, not only the confidence and the genuine support and respect of those whom they serve, but also their esteem and real affection. They must, at all times, avoid the spirit of exclusiveness, the atmosphere of secrecy, free themselves from a domineering attitude, and banish all forms of prejudice and passion from their deliberations. . . . And, when they are called upon to arrive at a certain decision, they should, after dispassionate, anxious, and cordial consultation, turn to God in prayer, and with earnestness and conviction and courage record their vote and abide by the voice of the majority. . . ."   (PBA 43-44)

Consultation

Consultation among the members of the Assembly is of utmost importance. In fact, Bahá'í Administration cannot function without consultation. There are two important factors which Bahá'ís must always remember. First, that every individual has the right to self-expression: he is free to declare his conscience and give his personal opinions. Second, that once he has expressed his views, he must not dogmatically cling to them with utter disregard for other people's opinions. He should always be prepared to look into ideas advanced by others and consult with them on every matter in a spirit of sincere fellowship. When the principle of consultation is carried out in an Assembly, the decision arrived at is usually very different, and far better than anything the individual members first had in mind when they started their discussions.

Having heard the views of each individual and consulted together about the matter in hand, the members of the Assembly very often arrive at a unanimous decision. If this does not happen, the vote of the majority becomes the decision of the Assembly. This decision is then whole-heartedly supported, not only by its members, but by the whole of the local Bahá'í community. No one should criticize the Assembly or act contrary to its decisions. The wisdom of this is clear, for if every Bahá'í wished to run the affairs of the community according to his own judgment, disorder would prevail and the spirit of unity would be completely destroyed. The individual has the right, however, to ask the Assembly to reconsider its decision if he is convinced that a grave mistake has been made.

'Abdu'l-Bahá explains the requisites of true consultation among the members of an Assembly:

"The members thereof must take counsel together in such wise that no occasion for ill-feeling or discord may arise. This can be attained when every member expresseth with absolute freedom his own opinion and setteth forth his argument. Should any one oppose, he must on no account feel hurt for not until matters are fully discussed can the right way be revealed.

95

The shining spark of truth cometh forth only after the clash of differing opinions. If, after discussion, a decision be carried unanimously, well and good; but if, the Lord forbid, differences of opinion should arise, a majority of voices must prevail.

"The first condition is absolute love and harmony amongst the members of the Assembly. . . . The second condition: They must, when coming together, turn their faces to the Kingdom on High and ask aid from the Realm of Glory. They must then proceed with the utmost devotion, courtesy, dignity, care, and moderation to express their views. They must in every matter search out the truth and not insist upon their own opinion, for stubbornness and persistence in one's views will lead ultimately to discord and wrangling and the truth will remain hidden. The honoured members must with all freedom express their own thoughts, and it is in no wise permissible for one to belittle the thought of another . . . and should differences of opinion arise a majority of voices must prevail, and all must obey and submit to the majority. . . .

". . . Discussions must all be confined to spiritual matters that pertain to the training of souls, the instruction of children, the relief of the poor, the help of the feeble throughout all classes in the world, kindness to all peoples, the diffusion of the fragrances of God, and the exaltation of His Holy Word. Should they endeavour to fulfil these conditions . . . that Assembly shall become the centre of the Divine blessings, the hosts of Divine confirmation shall come to their aid and they shall day by day receive a new effusion of Spirit." (PBA 41-43)

The Nineteen Day Feast

All the Bahá'ís in a community meet together at regular intervals to pray, to consult about their work, and to strengthen their ties of friendship. This gathering is called the Nineteen Day Feast because it takes place every nineteen days.

The Feast is divided into three parts. The first part consists of a devotional program of prayers from Bahá'í Scriptures. During the second part, the Spiritual Assembly reports on its activities to the community and consults with them about its work and problems. The chairman should see that all those who are present are given opportunity to express their views and take part in the consultation. Suggestions given at the Nineteen Day Feast are recorded by the secretary for careful consideration at the meeting of the Spiritual Assembly. In this way, every individual Bahá'í can contribute towards the running of the affairs of the community even if he is not a member of the Assembly, though the final decision rests on the elected body.

Letters, news, and reports received from other parts of the country and the world are also read and discussed during this period.

The third and last part of the Feast is purely

social. It is for the purpose of promoting unity and friendship among the members of the community.

Thousands of such gatherings are now being held, on the same day, in modern houses and mud huts, in skyscrapers, wigwams, and igloos, under the sky in a jungle clearing, or in the hall of a beautiful building. Wherever they may come together, whatever their color, language, or social standing, those taking part in a Nineteen Day Feast are all fully conscious that they are parts of a great Unity which nothing can destroy.

Bahá'í Calendar

Before going further with the Administration, let us stop to look at the dates on which the Nineteen Day Feasts are held.

There are many different types of calendars used throughout the world today, and none of these correspond with each other. Bahá'ís living in various communities make use of a new calendar which was inaugurated by the Báb. This calendar starts with the birth of the new Dispensation, and is divided into nineteen months of nineteen days, each month bearing the name of one of the attributes of God. Between the last two months, there are four intercalary days (five in leap years) in order to adjust the calendar to the solar year. The New Year is astronomically fixed and commences at the March equinox (usually March 21).

Nineteen Day Feasts are held on the first day of each of the following months:

Names of Months		First Days
1st	Splendor	March 21
2nd	Glory	April 9
3rd	Beauty	April 28
4th	Grandeur	May 17
5th	Light	June 5
6th	Mercy	June 24
7th	Words	July 13
8th	Perfection	August 1
9th	Names	August 20
10th	Might	September 8
11th	Will	September 27
12th	Knowledge	October 16
13th	Power	November 4
14th	Speech	November 23
15th	Questions	December 12
16th	Honor	December 31
17th	Sovereignty	January 19
18th	Dominion	February 7
	Intercalary Days	February 26-March 1
19th	Loftiness	March 2

The National Spiritual Assembly

The Local Spiritual Assemblies deal with the affairs of Bahá'ís in each town or village. There may be dozens or hundreds of Local Assemblies in one country. These Assemblies are under the jurisdiction of a National Spiritual Assembly which directs, stimulates, unifies, and coordinates the activities of all the Bahá'ís in that country.

Each year, local communities elect delegates from among themselves to attend a National

Convention, and these delegates elect nine
Bahá'ís from the whole country to serve on the
National Spiritual Assembly for that year. As in
every Bahá'í election, there is no nomination
or propaganda of any kind, and anyone who has
reached the age of twenty-one can be elected.
The delegates vote, by secret ballot, for those
who they conscientiously feel "can best combine
the necessary qualities of unquestioned loyalty,
of selfless devotion, of a well-trained mind, of
recognized ability and mature experience."

(PBA 63)

The authority of the National Assembly is
above that of Local Assemblies, and any decisions arrived at by a National Assembly are supported by all Local Assemblies within its jurisdiction. The National Assembly usually deals
with matters of national importance and leaves
the organization of affairs in each town or village
to the discretion of its own elected body, but it is
always ready to assist its Local Assemblies
should they require help and guidance. The decisions of the various Local Assemblies are report-
ed to the national body so that the National
Assembly is aware of the work going on in every
part of the country.

The National Assembly is also in touch with
the members of each community through
newsletters and other correspondence sent for the
Nineteen Day Feasts. Any suggestions coming
from these Feasts which concern the whole country are considered and consulted upon by the
National Assembly.

Bahá'ís who do not have a Local Assembly in the place they live communicate directly with their National Assembly who sends them news and guides their activities until they form their own Local Assembly.

Regarding the duties of the National Assembly towards the Bahá'ís whom they serve, the Guardian has written:

"Let it be made clear to every inquiring reader that among the most outstanding and sacred duties incumbent upon those who have been called upon to initiate, direct, and co-ordinate the affairs of the Cause, are those that require them to win by every means in their power the confidence and affection of those whom it is their privilege to serve. Theirs is the duty to investigate and acquaint themselves with the considered views, the prevailing sentiments, the personal convictions of those whose welfare it is their solemn obligation to promote. Theirs is the duty to purge once for all their deliberations and the general conduct of their affairs from that air of self-contained aloofness, from the suspicion of secrecy, the stifling atmosphere of dictatorial assertiveness, in short, from every word and deed that might savour of partiality, self-centredness, and prejudice. Theirs is the duty, while retaining the sacred and exclusive right of final decision in their hands, to invite discussion, provide information, ventilate grievances, welcome advice from even the most humble and insignificant members of the Bahá'í family, expose their motives, set forth their plans, justify their actions, revise if necessary their verdict, foster the sense of interdependence and co-partnership, of understanding and mutual confidence between them on one hand and all local Assemblies and individual believers on the other."

(PBA 79-80)

The Universal House of Justice

All the National Assemblies of the world come under the jurisdiction of an international body called The Universal House of Justice. Just as the National Assembly directs and unifies the Local Assemblies within its jurisdiction, the House of Justice guides and coordinates the activities of all the various National Assemblies of the world. The House of Justice gives plans and sets goals for the whole of the Bahá'í world, and the National Assemblies unitedly put those plans into action.

A main difference, however, between the House of Justice and the Assemblies is that Bahá'u'lláh has given this Supreme International Body the right to enact such laws as are not explicitly given by Himself. For example, Bahá'u'lláh teaches that capital should give a percentage of its profits to labor. He does not, however, say what that percentage should be because the amount may have to vary from time to time. The House of Justice, therefore, can decide on what that percentage should be; and if at some later date the rate of percentage has to be changed, the House of Justice can make that change. In other words, the House of Justice cannot alter any of the laws given by Bahá-u'lláh; but it can legislate on matters which He has left for it to decide on. The House of Justice can also change its own laws when the necessity arises.

There is another major difference between the House of Justice and all other Assemblies. Bahá'ís have been promised that the House of Justice will always be guided by God to make the right decisions.

When a Bahá'í feels that his Local Assembly has made a decision which is contrary to the Teachings of Bahá'u'lláh or is opposed to the best interests of His Cause, he can ask that Assembly to reconsider the matter. If he is not satisfied with the outcome, he can appeal to the National Assembly of the country in which he is living. From the National Assembly, he can make a further appeal to The Universal House of Justice. The decision of the House of Justice, however, is accepted as final by every Bahá'í.

The first Universal House of Justice was elected in 1963 at an International Convention held at the World Centre of the Bahá'í Faith in the Holy Land. It was immediately after this historic election that thousands of Bahá'ís, coming from every part of the world, met at the Albert Hall in London to celebrate the centenary of Bahá'u'lláh's Declaration.

Loyalty to Government

The institutions of the Bahá'í Faith in their present form are chiefly concerned with spreading the Teachings of Bahá'u'lláh, preserving the unity of His followers, and coordinating their humanitarian activities throughout the planet.

Bahá'ís believe that the peoples of the world will come to accept the principles of the Administrative Order given by Bahá'u'lláh as the pattern for the future World Commonwealth. Until that time, however, they must be loyal and obedient to the laws of the land in which they live. Bahá'u'lláh says:

"In every country where any of this community reside, they must behave toward the government of that country with faithfulness, truthfulness and obedience."
(BNE 147)

'Abdu'l-Bahá further explains:

"We must obey and be the well-wishers of the governments of the land, regard disloyalty unto a just king as disloyalty to God Himself and wishing evil to the government a transgression of the Cause of God."
(BR 308)

Bahá'ís are only justified in refusing to cooperate with a government when they are called upon to do something which would be a departure from the principle of loyalty to their Faith. They cannot, for example, help in exterminating a minority group because of their color or religious convictions; nor can they side with one political party against another, as this will destroy the unity which they have established throughout the world and which rises above all racial, religious, and political differences between people. But they willingly obey the laws of the government in all matters which do not amount to a recantation of their Faith.

Hands of the Cause of God

Bahá'u'lláh, during His own lifetime, chose certain of His trusted followers to give their special assistance to the work of the Faith. He designated them as "Hands of the Cause of God." In His Will and Testament, 'Abdu'l-Bahá made provisions for the Guardian to appoint Hands of the Cause to help him in the enormous task entrusted to his care. The Guardian chose a number of men and women from Bahá'ís all over the world, and many of these Hands of the Cause are still living and carrying on with the duties allotted to them.

The Hands of the Cause are not elected to the administrative institutions of the Faith, but they work in close collaboration with The Universal House of Justice and obey its decisions.

Unity among Bahá'ís

From what has been mentioned about Bahá'í Administration, it is clear that individual members of every community in the world have the right to voice their opinions, vote for their Local and National Assemblies, and be elected to them. Through those whom they choose as members of the National Assemblies, they also indirectly elect The Universal House of Justice.

Having elected their administrative institutions, Bahá'ís are encouraged to provide them with fresh ideas and suggestions for the progress of their work, but final decisions are arrived at by the elected bodies. The Local Assemblies are responsible to their National Assembly, and all the National Assemblies of the world are responsible to the House of Justice. In this way, the unity of the Bahá'í Faith is preserved, because it is impossible for a person to be a follower of Bahá'u'lláh and refuse to accept His Administrative Order.

If an individual calls himself a Bahá'í but openly violates the principles laid down by Bahá'u'lláh, no member of the community can rebuke him; but his Local or National Assembly must, with wisdom and kindness, help him to see his mistake and change his attitude. If, however, having done all it can for him, the National Assembly decides that the individual is consciously harming the reputation of the Bahá'í Community, it has the right to deprive him of his administrative rights. This means that he will not be given the full rights other Bahá'ís enjoy such as voting for or being elected to Bahá'í institutions until such time as he is prepared to mend his ways.

Bahá'u'lláh says that the greatest harm anyone can do to His Cause is to call himself a believer in Bahá'u'lláh and then try to introduce disunity among His followers. This is a very grave departure from the tenets of a Faith which is based on unity and strives to set an example of unity through its own followers.

To protect His Cause from splitting into sects, Bahá'u'lláh made a Covenant with His followers that after Him they should all turn to 'Abdu'l-Bahá for guidance. And 'Abdu'l-Bahá renewed this Covenant with the Bahá'ís by asking them to obey Shoghi Effendi and the Universal House of Justice. Shoghi Effendi has now passed away, but The House of Justice will go on to the end of the Bahá'í Dispensation which, Bahá'u'lláh said, would last at least one thousand years.

Anyone who calls himself a Bahá'í but refuses to obey the House of Justice has broken the Covenant of Bahá'u'lláh and, by setting up his own authority above that of the House of Justice, is trying to introduce a breach within the ranks of the Bahá'ís. To prevent this, the followers of Bahá'u'lláh are instructed to have nothing whatsoever to do with him. In this way alone will such a person, who is referred to as a Covenant-breaker, be prevented from doing any harm to the unity of the Faith. If he later repents his behavior and announces his loyalty to the House of Justice, he can join the Bahá'í community once again.

A person who has been a Bahá'í but then changes his mind and does not wish to be known as a member of the Faith anymore, is not, of course, a Covenant-breaker. Bahá'ís will continue to associate with him without any hesitation. Only if a person insists that he is a follower of Bahá'u'lláh, then tries to create a split among the members of the Faith by working against the House of Justice, will the Bahá'ís of the world refuse to associate with him. The wisdom of this has already been shown in the past. The most significant example occurred when a few of the close relatives of Bahá-'u'lláh Himself, because of their physical relationship with the Founder of the Faith, imagined that they could become leaders in this Cause and form a following for themselves. As soon as they set out to belittle the Covenant which Bahá-'u'lláh had made with His followers and refused to acknowledge the authority of 'Abdu'l-Bahá, the Bahá'ís of the world refused to have anything to do with them and the few people whom they had managed to mislead. The result was that some of these people came to realize their mistake and joined the Bahá'ís once more, while the rest gradually faded away and left no trace.

The unity of this infant Faith has been put to the test more than once in the past, and each time it has emerged from the trial stronger than before.

Houses of Worship

According to the instructions of Bahá'u'lláh, a House of Worship should be erected in every locality so that people can assemble to worship God together no matter what their religious beliefs may be. In these Houses of Worship, readings are taken from the sacred Scriptures of the world. As there are no priests in the Bahá'í Faith, the program of readings is arranged by a committee and carried out by ordinary men and women. No one gives a sermon or conducts any form of ceremony or ritual. Lectures, discussions, or study classes on the Bahá'í Faith and other religions must take place elsewhere because the House of Worship is reserved for prayer and meditation.

The style of the architecture of these buildings may vary, but there are certain features which all the Houses of Worship have in common. For example, they are nine-sided with doors opening on every side. The number nine is a symbol of unity because all other digits are included in nine; the fact that the building has no back signifies that its doors are open to all mankind. Houses of Worship must be surrounded by beautiful gardens and a number of other buildings devoted to educational, social, and charitable purposes so that the worship of God may be associated with the beauty of nature and practical service to fellowmen.

Up to this date, the Bahá'ís have been able to construct a House of Worship in each of the five continents, and over fifty other sites have been bought for future buildings in various parts of the world.

Funds

The financial demands of an ever-growing world community are met through local, national, and international funds. These funds come from voluntary contributions by members of the Faith. No money is accepted from those who do not believe in Bahá'u'lláh, and His followers are free to give for whatever purpose they wish and however much they can afford. No one is informed of the amount different individuals contribute to the funds.

Bahá'ís consider it a great privilege to be called upon to serve the cause of Unity, and giving from their material resources is a practical way in which they all support this Cause.

Holy Days

The Bahá'í Faith is a joyous and happy Faith. The great joy of life which Bahá'ís feel finds a united expression on seven days of festivity throughout the year. Speaking on one of these days, 'Abdu'l-Bahá said:

"In the sacred laws of God, in every cycle and dispensation there are blessed feasts, holidays and workless days.

"On such days all kinds of occupations, commerce, industry, agriculture, et cetera, should be suspended.

"All should rejoice together, hold general meetings, become as one assembly, so that the national oneness, unity and harmony may be demonstrated in the eyes of all.

"As it is a blessed day it should not be neglected, nor deprived of results by making it a day devoted to the pursuit of mere pleasure.

"During such days institutions should be founded that may be of permanent benefit and value to the people. . . .

". . . Undoubtedly the friends of God, upon such a day, must leave tangible philanthropic or ideal traces that should reach all mankind and not pertain only to the Bahá'ís." (BNE 187-88)

There are nine days in each year on which Bahá'ís refrain from work. Seven are joyous festivals, and the two others commemorate the martyrdom of the Báb and the passing of Bahá'u'lláh. They are in this order:

March 21. New Year's Day. This is also the day on which the period of fasting ends.

April 21, April 29, May 2. The most important festival period among Bahá'ís is during the twelve days which Bahá'u'lláh spent in the garden of Ridván, outside Baghdád, before His exile to Constantinople. This was the time when He openly declared His Mission. The first, the ninth, and the twelfth are days on which work is suspended.

May 23. The Declaration of the Báb, when He revealed His Mission to His first disciple.

May 29. The passing of Bahá'u'lláh, which took place in the Holy Land.

July 9. The martyrdom of the Báb.

October 20. The birth of the Báb.

November 12. The birth of Bahá'u'lláh.

There are two other Anniversaries, both associated with 'Abdu'l-Bahá, which are of importance to Bahá'ís, but these are not considered as Holy Days on which work should be suspended. The first, November 26, is known as the Day of the Covenant. On this day, Bahá'ís celebrate the appointment of 'Abdu'l-Bahá as the Center of Bahá'u'lláh's Covenant with His followers. The second, November 28, marks the day when 'Abdu'l-Bahá passed away.

Joining the Bahá'í Community

Many people who are aware of the high standards set by Bahá'u'lláh feel that they can never live up to these ideals, and are therefore unable to call themselves Bahá'ís. The truth is that among all the followers of Bahá'u'lláh, only one man lived the perfect life of a Bahá'í, and that was 'Abdu'l-Bahá. Bahá'ís are well aware of their shortcomings, and this is one of the reasons why they feel they need the help of Bahá'u'lláh. For the purpose of God in sending His Messenger is to help men at the time of their greatest need.

The divine Physician comes to give the remedy for men's illness of heart and soul. Those who recognize the Physician will want to start taking His prescription, knowing full well that if they have courage and perseverance, the divine remedy will bring gradual health and happiness, not only for themselves, but for all the human family of which they are a part.

When a person believes in Bahá'u'lláh as the Messenger of God for this age, he is a Bahá'í. He does not need to change his name or go through any kind of ceremony. For administrative records and practical reasons, he is expected to declare his faith to the Local Assembly of the place in which he lives. If there is no Local Assembly in his town or village, he notifies the National Assembly of the country he is living in at the time.

As a member of the Bahá'í community, he is then ready to join forces with his fellow-believers scattered throughout the world and work for the unity of mankind.

SELECTIONS
FROM
THE WRITINGS OF BAHÁ'U'LLÁH

The world's equilibrium hath been upset through the vibrating influence of this most great, this new World Order. Mankind's ordered life hath been revolutionized through the agency of this unique, this wondrous System—the like of which mortal eyes have never witnessed.
(GWB 136)

A new life is, in this age, stirring within all the peoples of the earth; and yet none hath discovered its cause or perceived its motive. . . .

O friends! Be not careless of the virtues with which ye have been endowed, neither be neglectful of your high destiny. Suffer not your labors to be wasted through the vain imaginations which certain hearts have devised. Ye are the stars of the heaven of understanding, the breeze that stirreth at the break of day, the soft-flowing waters upon which must depend the very life of all men. . . .

Be ye guided by wisdom in all your doings,

and cleave ye tenaciously unto it. Please God ye may all be strengthened to carry out that which is the Will of God, and may be graciously assisted to appreciate the rank conferred upon such of His loved ones as have arisen to serve Him and magnify His name.   (GWB 196-97)

The Book of God is wide open, and His Word is summoning mankind unto Him. No more than a mere handful, however, hath been found willing to cleave to His Cause, or to become the instruments for its promotion. . . .
Incline your ears, O friends of God, to the voice of Him Whom the world hath wronged, and hold fast unto whatsoever will exalt His Cause. . . . This is a Revelation that infuseth strength into the feeble, and crowneth with wealth the destitute.
With the utmost friendliness and in a spirit of perfect fellowship take ye counsel together, and dedicate the precious days of your lives to the betterment of the world and the promotion of the Cause of Him Who is the Ancient and Sovereign Lord of all.   (GWB 183-84)

The men of the House of Justice of God must, night and day, gaze toward that which hath been revealed from the horizon of the heaven of the Supreme Pen for the training of the servants, for the upbuilding of countries, for the protection of men and for the preservation of human honour.
(BR 156)

Address yourselves to the promotion of the

well-being and tranquillity of the children of men. Bend your minds and wills to the education of the peoples and kindreds of the earth, that haply the dissensions that divide it may, through the power of the Most Great Name, be blotted out from its face, and all mankind become the upholders of one Order, and the inhabitants of one City. (GWB 333-34)

They whom God hath endued with insight will readily recognize that the precepts laid down by God constitute the highest means for the maintenance of order in the world and the security of its peoples. . . .

O ye peoples of the world! Know assuredly that My commandments are the lamps of My loving providence among My servants, and the keys of My mercy for My creatures. . . .

Think not that We have revealed unto you a mere code of laws. Nay, rather, We have unsealed the choice Wine with the fingers of might and power. To this beareth witness that which the Pen of Revelation hath revealed. Meditate upon this, O men of insight! . . .

(GWB 331-33)

Every word that proceedeth out of the mouth of God is endowed with such potency as can instill new life into every human frame, if ye be of them that comprehend this truth. All the wondrous works ye behold in this world have been manifested through the operation of His supreme and most exalted Will, His wondrous and inflexible Purpose. . . . In the days to come, ye will, verily, behold things of which ye have never heard before. (GWB 141-42)

When the victory arriveth, every man shall profess himself as believer and shall hasten to the shelter of God's Faith. Happy are they who in the days of world-encompassing trials have stood fast in the Cause and refused to swerve from its truth. (GWB 319)

O my God! O my God! Unite the hearts of Thy servants, and reveal to them Thy great purpose. May they follow Thy commandments and abide in Thy law. Help them, O God, in their endeavor, and grant them strength to serve Thee. O God! leave them not to themselves, but guide their steps by the light of knowledge, and cheer their hearts by Thy love. Verily, Thou art their Helper and their Lord. (BP 111)

BOOKS FOR FURTHER READING

In this brief introduction to the Bahá'í Faith, only a general picture has been given of how the Faith started, what Bahá'u'lláh taught, and how His followers are now working together throughout the world. It has not been possible, in a book of this size, to dwell at length on any particular aspect of the Faith, and many topics of importance have been only briefly touched upon. There are, however, a number of other Bahá'í books which deal with different subjects in far greater detail, and a list of some of these is given below. A complete catalogue of Bahá'í literature can be obtained from Bahá'í Publishing Trusts.

Gleanings from the Writings of Bahá'u'lláh. Excerpts from the Writings of Bahá'u'lláh, touching on the nature of religion, the spiritual nature of man, and the transformation of human society. 346 pp.

The Book of Certitude. Bahá'u'lláh sets forth the grand redemptive scheme of God, revealing the oneness of religion, its continuity and evolution through the successive Prophets of God, and elucidates some of the allegorical and abstruse passages of the Jewish, Christian, and Muslim Scriptures. 257 pp.

The Hidden Words of Bahá'u'lláh. The essence of all revealed truth, expressed in brief penetrating meditations. 52 pp.

Bahá'í World Faith. A comprehensive selection of the Writings of Bahá'u'lláh and 'Abdu'l-Bahá dealing with the mission of the Prophets, the fulfilment of religious promises, the nature of the soul and spirit of man, practices and laws for the new age. 449 pp.

The Divine Art of Living. Selections from the Writings of Bahá'u'lláh and Abdu'l-Bahá. Characterizes wholeness of living and the goals of spiritual development. 128 pp.

Bahá'í Prayers (General). A selection of prayers revealed by the Báb, Bahá'u'lláh, and 'Abdu'l-Bahá. 112 pp.

Paris Talks. Addresses given by 'Abdu'l-Bahá in Paris. Clear, simple, short chapters about Bahá'í Teachings and fundamental things of life. 184 pp.

The Pattern of Bahá'í Life. A compilation from Bahá'í Scripture with some passages from the writings of the Guardian. 61 pp.

God Passes By, Shoghi Effendi. This book recreates the scenes and events of the first hundred years of the Bahá'í Dispensation.   412 pp.

Bahá'u'lláh, H. M. Balyuzi. The book offers, in its first part, a short account of the earthly life of Bahá'u'lláh. The second part is an essay on the eternal Manifestation of God, that Divine Spirit Who, for a mortal span, occupies the human temple of Bahá'u'lláh, of Jesus of Nazareth, of Muḥammad, of Gautama.   130 pp.

'Abdu'l-Bahá, H. M. Balyuzi. A comprehensive biography of the One appointed by Bahá'u'lláh as the Center of His Covenant and the Interpreter and Exemplar of His Teachings.   495 pp.

Release the Sun, W. Sears. A moving, historical account of the mission and martyrdom of the Báb, the Herald of the Bahá'í Faith. The appendix gives extensive affirmation of biblical prophecies concerning the coming of the Báb and Bahá'u'lláh.   238 pp.

Portals to Freedom, H. C. Ives. A former Unitarian clergyman describes his meeting with 'Abdu'l-Bahá and the spiritual experiences that followed. The book contains the story of 'Abdu'l-Bahá's visit to America.   253 pp.

Prescription for Living, R. Rabbani. A Bahá'í approach to intimate problems of everyday life.   204 pp.

The Promise of All Ages, G. Townshend. A

biblical scholar and former Episcopalian clergyman traces the spiritual content of religion through the Dispensations of the past, to culminate in the World Order revealed by Bahá'u'lláh.   164 pp.

Tomorrow and Tomorrow, S. Cobb. A vivid picture of the future and the focusing of world trends that will eventuate in a peaceful, planetary society.   82 pp.

Bahá'u'lláh and the New Era, J. E. Esslemont. A standard introductory textbook, outlining the history and Teachings of the Faith. This book has been translated into fifty-eight languages. 286 pp.

ABBREVIATIONS

The following abbreviations are used for books from which passages have been selected.

B   Bahá'u'lláh (1963)

BNE   Bahá'u'lláh and the New Era (American paper edition, 1970)

BP   Bahá'í Prayers (American edition, 1970)

BR   The Bahá'í Revelation (1955)

BWF   Bahá'í World Faith (1969)

DB   The Dawn-Breakers (American edition, 1962)

ESW   Epistle to the Son of the Wolf (American edition, 1969)

GWB   Gleanings from the Writings of Bahá'u'lláh (American edition, 1952)

HW   The Hidden Words (American edition, 1954)

PBA   Principles of Bahá'í Administration (1963)

PBL   The Pattern of Bahá'í Life (1968)